EDUCATION ANSWERS BACK

Dedicated to the memory of
HARRY RÉE, DSO OBE
True and consistent fighter
for education; powered by a
full humanity
in thought and action

EDUCATION ANSWERS BACK

Critical Responses to Government Policy

Edited and Introduced by
Brian Simon and Clyde Chitty

LAWRENCE & WISHART
LONDON

Lawrence & Wishart Ltd
144a Old South Lambeth Road
London SW8 1XX

First published in 1993

ISBN 0 85315 781 2

Cover and text designed by
Jan Brown Designs, London.
Photoset in North Wales by
Derek Doyle Associates, Mold, Clwyd.
Printed and bound in Great Britain by
Dotesios Ltd, Trowbridge, Wilts.

CONTENTS

CONTENTS

ACKNOWLEDGEMENTS

Our thanks are due to many for permission to reproduce several of the documents in this book. To the British Education Research Association for permission to reproduce extracts from Dr Gipps' presidential address; to the British Association for permission to reproduce Denis Lawton's, Peter Watkins' and Jim Campbell's addresses, all delivered at the British Association's annual conference at Southampton in August 1992; to the *Times Educational Supplement* for permission to reproduce Stuart Maclure's article of 4 September 1992 and that of Margaret Maden of 25 September 1992; to the *Observer* for Duncan Graham's article of 6 September 1992; to the *Independent on Sunday*, for Judith Judd and Ngaio Crequer's article of 2 August 1992; to the Conservative Central Office for John Major and John Patten's speeches to the Conservative Party Conference in October 1992; to Fred Jarvis for items of his correspondence with the Prime Minister; to *The Times* for its leader of 29 July 1992; and to the *Observer* for Barry Hugill's article of 2 August 1992. Our thanks are due also to Eric Bolton and Paul Black for permission to reproduce their addresses to the Council of Local Education Authorities and to the British Association respectively.

ABBREVIATIONS

APU	Assessment of Performance Unit
CBI	Confederation of British Industry
CFF	Common Funding Formula
CSE	Certificate of Secondary Education
DES	Department of Education and Science
DFE	Department For Education
ERA	Education Reform Act (1988)
GCE	General Certificate of Education
GCSE	General Certificate of Secondary Education
GMS	Grant Maintained School
GTC	General Teaching Council
HMI	Her Majesty's Inspector
ITT	Initial Teacher Training
JMB	Joint Matriculation Board
LEA	Local Education Authority
LMS	Local Management of Schools
LSE	London School of Economics
NCC	National Curriculum Council
NCVQ	National Council for Vocational Qualifications
SAT	Standard Assessment Task
SEAC	School Examinations and Assessment Council
SEN	Special Educational Needs
SSA	Standard Spending Assessment
TGAT	Task Group for Assessment and Testing

INTRODUCTION

Over the summer of 1992, prestigious audiences were presented with a number of very striking addresses severely critical of current developments in education and particularly of its continual politicisation. Those speaking were aware that yet another massive Education Bill was to be presented to Parliament shortly, preceded by a White Paper. All felt it incumbent on them to add their voices to those warning the Government against some of the crucial tendencies in government policy now becoming increasingly apparent.

One feature of this barrage (for this is what it became) was the fact that most of those participating had, through intensive work often under great difficulties, done their very best to ensure that Kenneth Baker's 1988 Education Act, which had aroused widespread opposition at the time, was given a fair chance to operate successfully. Eric Bolton, as Senior Chief Inspector from 1983 to 1991, fully co-operated with government intentions, as was, of course, his duty. All the more impressive, therefore, were the very serious warnings he offered on that policy, and its centres of inspiration, in his address to the annual conference of the Council of Local Education Authorities (CLEA) which we reproduce as our first item. There is no crime in listening to your political friends, Bolton concludes, 'but a wise government listens more widely than that.' The danger of listening so selectively is that the Government fails to recognise the new reality which 'may be more akin, as Tacitus put it long ago, to the Government "making a wilderness and calling it peace".'

This was a powerful warning delivered with due seriousness and in a calm and measured manner. Equally impressive, however, was Professor Paul Black's address a month later to the Education Section of the British Association for the Advancement of Science. As is very well known, Professor Black was the original Chair of the Task Group for Assessment and Testing (TGAT) whose report, without any doubt whatsoever, played the crucial role in winning the educational world (and particularly teachers) to a more sympathetic view of the Education Reform Act (1988). Developments, outlined in detail in his speech, since that time – especially the arrogation of all powers to the centre – have led Professor Black to the conclusion that 'Those who gave dire warnings that the Education Reform Act would be an instrument for direct government control in which the opinions of ministers would be insulated from professional opinion and expertise have been proved correct.' Both Paul Black and Eric Bolton point to the ominous increase in the strength of the extreme right wing of the Tory Party in decision-making as the most disquieting feature of the present scene.

We are proud and glad to reproduce these two courageous addresses in this volume. Both received widespread publicity at the time, in both the national and educational press, but neither has been reproduced in full before; and, in any case, instant publicity is soon forgotten. Because we feel both statements have a historic significance, we felt it absolutely necessary to reproduce them in this volume, and are very grateful to both Eric Bolton and Paul Black for their full co-operation.

But there are others too who have raised their voices in protest. Chief among these must be rated Duncan Graham, the first Chair and Chief Executive of the National Curriculum Council (NCC) who also tried, in his own way, to implement government policy effectively in the sphere of curriculum change. In July 1991, owing specifically to what were largely political pressures, he was forced to resign his appointment. Some of the factors which brought about his resignation are referred to in the article we reproduce here. Since going to press, Duncan Graham has published his own version of these events in his recent book, *A Lesson For Us All*.

Because of its relevance, we also reproduce Peter Watkins' address given at Birmingham University at the end of November 1991. Mr Watkins was Duncan Graham's deputy at the National Curriculum Council until his resignation in 1991, and so was fully involved in assisting the Government in making its curriculum policy – which, as he makes clear, he personally fully supported – a success. Very serious problems have arisen, however, and these Mr Watkins reviews, proposing solutions. But he is also primarily concerned with the impact of the overt politicisation now apparent. 'Now, however,' he writes, 'the independence of the Council and that of SEAC is in jeopardy'. 'The Councils', he goes on, 'seem to be regarded by the Government not as sources of independent, authoritative advice but are used to endorse and set out in detail what the Secretary of State has already decided to do.' Several cavalier ministerial decisions are referred to at the end of his impressive lecture. But, he adds, 'The enterprise is too important to be compromised by political partisanship or point-scoring by pressure groups.' If this continues the momentum will be lost, together with any chance of ensuring the raised standards which are at least the overt objective. This also is a serious warning.

Reference has, in fact, been made to some of the most important contributions in this volume, but – we would claim – all are important, and all bear on crucial issues now under discussion. The book is arranged in three main parts. Part I comprises Eric Bolton's address, and Caroline Gipps' presidential address to the annual conference of the British Education Research Association (BERA) held at the end of August 1992. As a research body BERA is particularly concerned about the accurate use of research findings, and Dr Gipps draws attention to the blatant abuse of this principle by government ministers when in pursuit of quick political advantage. This, of course, lowers the whole level of educational discussion and totally confuses important issues in the mind of the public. Dr Gipps' contribution is, therefore, both important and closely relevant.

The other item in Part I is Anne Corbett's up-to-the-minute assessment of England's comparative position in education compared to other advanced European countries. She penetrates into the historical roots of English backwardness in education and stresses the urgent need for constructive action, particularly in the area of the sixteen to nineteen age group and in pre-school provision (neither of which even rates a mention either in the White Paper or in the Education Bill itself).

Part II focuses specifically on the national curriculum and assessment, beginning with Paul Black's address already discussed, and including both Duncan Graham's assessment and the address by Peter Watkins, also already mentioned. In Chapter 5, however, Professor Denis Lawton, one of the leading curriculum theorists in the country, contributes his own short address to the British Association Education Section in August 1992. His own analysis leads him to the conclusion that, while the national curriculum was a tremendous opportunity, 'it was a missed opportunity,' largely because its top-down, bureaucratic imposition meant that teachers were treated as 'hirelings to be given instructions rather than as professionals to be involved at all stages and at all levels'. Denis Lawton also warns strongly against reliance on the 'quick fix' type of solution favoured by politicians to meet self-serving or short-term political objectives. He also warns strongly against current tendencies: 'Politicians', he concludes, 'have a legitimate interest in the curriculum, but when it comes to making the system work they should be guided by those who know something about it rather than by the ill-informed, extremist views of political advisers.'

At the same British Association at which Paul Black and Denis Lawton spoke, Professor Jim Campbell, a specialist on primary education, gave an extended and very constructive address on the national curriculum in primary schools, a phenomenon he describes as 'A Dream at Conception' but 'a Nightmare on Delivery'. Here he makes clear, basing himself on recent research which he and others have carried out, that the full national curriculum imposes impossible tasks on primary schools and teachers. He finishes by proposing various possible solutions, though all, he admits, are controversial. We are glad to include this as a balanced and well grounded discussion of what is, in fact, a very serious and difficult problem. We can hardly expect our primary teachers as a whole to become the equivalent of Albert Einstein, Marie Curie and Linford Christie 'rolled into one', as Jim Campbell puts it.

In Part III we include contributions of a rather different kind, though closely relevant to the general issues under discussion. Stuart Maclure brings his cool analytic mind to bear on the White Paper's confusions relating to policy for grant maintained schools (Chapter 9), while Margaret Maden presents her view from within the increasingly embattled local education authorities (Chapter 10). In view of the increasing concern of responsible people about the clearly growing influence of right-wing extremism in the Government we include an analysis of these forces by Judith Judd and Ngaio Crequer of the *Independent on Sunday*. We also include items from the long-running correspondence on educational policy between Fred Jarvis (formerly Secretary of the National Union of Teachers) and the Prime Minister, including the lengthy but succinct comments on government policy which comprise Mr Jarvis's last letter (25 September 1992) at the time of going to press. The Conservative Party Conference in October 1992 gave John Patten an opportunity for a reasoned defence of his policy as set out in the White Paper and forthcoming Education Bill; we have, therefore, reproduced his speech so that readers can judge for themselves what he made of it. The 300 words the Prime Minister devoted to education on that occasion are also included. Finally, in the Appendix, we have included *The Times'* main leader on the White

Paper, together with a comment on that document – by Barry Hugill of the *Observer*.

The materials in this book were brought together at very short notice in a week or so at the end of October 1992. If speed of production has led to errors we apologise, and, of course, must take full responsibility. We would like to thank all the contributors who generally entered enthusiastically into the project and gave it every support. In particular, we acknowledge the help given us by Anne Corbett, in discussion with whom the idea of this book took shape, and who, in the midst of a busy schedule, wrote especially for us the chapter in Part I mentioned above. This was the only piece purposely written for the book, and strengthens it immeasurably. We would also like to thank our publishers, Lawrence & Wishart – specifically Sally Davison and her team; without their enthusiastic support this volume would probably never have seen the light of day. Thanks also are due to them for giving the book, taken on at very short notice, full priority in order to ensure publication in time to influence proceedings in Parliament.

As editors we have kept a low profile in this volume, conceiving our job as facilitators to ensure expression of the views of others. We intend to present our own analysis, and critique, of the Education Bill in another publication, also through Lawrence & Wishart, entitled *SOS: Save Our Schools*, which we expect to be published shortly after this volume.

When this book was already in print (at the proof stage), Sir Malcolm Thornton, Chairman of the House of Commons Select Committee on Education, Science and the Arts, delivered a striking address to an audience of headteachers and academics at the De Montfort University, Leicester (on 3 December 1992). This, we felt, was very relevant indeed to one of the main themes of this book (the growing influence of extremist right-wing advisers on Government ministers and policy), as well as to other, related matters of concern, for instance, the role of local government. We are grateful, therefore, to Sir Malcolm and the University for permission to reproduce this address in full in this volume.

Brian Simon and Clyde Chitty
15 December 1992

PART I

1

IMAGINARY GARDENS WITH REAL TOADS

ERIC BOLTON, CB MA

Eric Bolton retired from his post as Senior Chief Inspector of schools in 1991. He is now Professor of Teacher Education at the Institute of Education, University of London.

This address was delivered at the annual conference of the Council of Local Education Authorities at Liverpool on 20 July 1992, just before the publication of the White Paper, 'Choice and Diversity, a New Framework for Schools'. This address was widely reported both in the national and educational press, but it has not previously been reproduced in full.

The title of my talk 'Imaginary Gardens with Real Toads' comes from the poet Marianne Moore. I use it, in part, because in 1976 my predecessor as Senior Chief Inspector, Sheila Browne, talked to the annual conference of CLEA. The title of her talk was 'The Secret Garden' and its gist was that the school curriculum had to be opened up to the wider influence of all who had a legitimate interest in it: the government, parents, employers; not just teachers and 'educationists'. It occurred to me, sixteen years on, that we did not sufficiently recognise, then, all that would be let loose in the curriculum when that magical, secret garden was opened up: we ignored the 'real toads'.

Towards the end of the Vietnam War the Vietcong suddenly launched a series of urban offensives and for a week or so took effective control of the centre of Saigon and a number of other Vietnamese cities. The American high command was badly shaken by such a display of strength. At a press conference, and under great media pressure, an American general complained desperately that, 'The future is not what it was!'

Certainly, in education the future is not what it was. If we put ourselves back to the early 1970s, the perception of the future of the education service was one in which there seemed to be every prospect of an ever-growing pupil population; the national government somewhat distantly concerned itself with teacher supply, loan sanctions for school building programmes and with tit-for-tat arguments with the opposition about comprehensive reorganisation. LEAs were busy building the schools; appointing teachers; providing nursery education; catering for new immigrant populations and providing courses for serving teachers. The schools were busy curriculum developing; the primary school curriculum expanded massively; secondary schools saw the raising of the school leaving age to 16, the increase in comprehensive schooling and curriculum development in most academic subjects.

There is a risk in retrospect that it begins to have all the appearance of a 'golden age'. It did not feel like that at the time. There were problems and difficulties aplenty. This is not the place to rehearse those, but it is the time to emphasise that most people in education then saw the future as a more-or-less smooth continuation of the present. A future in which the government would keep out of the way and teachers and 'educationists' would get on with the important business of determining, delivering and evaluating what went on in schools.

Around that time (the early 1970s), Mrs Thatcher, then the Secretary of State for Education, produced her White Paper, *A Framework For Expansion*. It was an important policy statement dealing with teacher supply, pre-school education and school building among other things. It is interesting to note here that it did not make any references to quality, standards or the curriculum.

But the world was changing. The early signs of the forthcoming dramatic fall in pupil numbers were beginning to show; a fall that would reduce the pupil population by a third on average and by as much as 40 per cent in some inner-urban areas. The Black Papers on education were published, raising questions about standards and questioning the educational orthodoxies of the day. The Schools Council's *Enquiry One* raised serious questions about the relevance of the curriculum to the world of work, employment and adult life, but it was largely ignored at the time.

By 1976 matters had developed to the point where the Prime Minister, James Callaghan, devoted the whole of a speech he gave at Ruskin College to education. Prime Ministers do not choose the topics for their speeches lightly, and by the time something is included it is already considered to be a serious and fairly widely accepted concern. Unlike 'A Framework for Expansion' a mere three or four years before, the Ruskin speech did deal with questions about the school curriculum and standards of achievement.

There was much shock-horror from the educational world at the Government claiming a national interest in what was taught in schools and launching the so-called 'Great Debate' about education. Shirley Williams asked all LEAs what their local arrangements for determining and overseeing the school curricula were. The search was on as to who, if anyone, was responsible and/or accountable for the school curriculum. Oddly, the answer seemed to be that no one was.

From then on the pace quickened. HMI reports on national standards and curricular provision in secondary and primary schools and some international comparative studies raised further worries about the quality and relevance to the modern world of much of what was going on inside our schools. Those worries were taken seriously by the Conservative Government of Mrs Thatcher that came to power in 1979. By 1985, Lord Joseph (Sir Keith Joseph as he then was), had taken the debate about quality, standards and the school curriculum much further. In his speech to the North of England Education Conference, and his subsequent White Paper, 'Better Schools', he set out what the Government thought the curriculum should be and called for standards of achievement to be raised at every level.

In 1988, twelve years after Callaghan's Ruskin speech, Kenneth Baker steered the Education Reform Act (ERA) onto the statute book. It is that Act, its implementation and its implications that are now taking up much of our time and energy. In the helter-skelter of that turbulent here-and-now, it is important to remember that there were, and are, well founded concerns about quality and standards in our education service. That the giant, national stocktaking in education in which we are involved was generated by a combination of concern about standards, coupled with a need to review and reflect upon the large-scale change and development that had taken place in education since the end of the 1950s.

It is also important to recognise that the ERA is, by conscious design, as well as by accident, an Act of two distinct halves with an in-built instability. One half, namely, the legislation concerned with the national curriculum and its related assessment arrangements is clearly a direct continuation of the professional debate about the curriculum begun back in the early 1970s. The other half has more to do with the Thatcher Government's macro-philosophy that efficiency and quality are best sustained and enhanced in situations where users and customers have choice, and the information and scope to use it as they decide – in other words, where there is a market. In that market clients and customers rule and any gathering of professionals or experts is, by definition almost, bound to be a conspiracy against the consumer. Grant maintained schools, local management of schools (LMS), open enrolment, public reporting of assessment results and league tables are all products of that thinking.

The Schools Act of 1992 has extended that thinking to school inspection by effectively de-coupling quality assurance from those responsible for the governance and administration of the education service; placing it in a kind of market, and insisting that every inspection must contain one inspector at least whose qualification is to know absolutely nothing about education!

So, where does all that leave us? 'In a mess' some of you will reply if you remain polite. But, more seriously, the various components of the ERA are working their ways into the system with varying degrees of success and difficulty. We will not have firm grounds for judgement about many developments for some time to come, partly because the timescales of change and development in education are much longer than are those of Secretaries of State and governments. It is already clear that the main *demandeurs* in the education service are now central government and the highly autonomous, individual schools.

The Government is now involved in much more than laying down general regulations for the curriculum and the broad framework within which schools should operate. It is increasingly active in the detailed organisation of what is happening on the ground.

For example, it is the Government that is determining the detailed arrangements for the publication of assessment results at local level. Even where the Government does not see its own civil servants directly involved in an activity, for example in the inspection of schools, it is extremely reluctant to leave any of those arrangements to the local education authorities. In fact, while the Government's overall intentions for the education service are somewhat opaque, it is crystal clear that it has no intention of increasing the responsibilities and duties of LEAs in the governance and administration of the education service.

There is no reason in principle why a state education service need have within it bodies such as LEAs. Quite a number of other countries run wholly respectable national educational services that get on quite well without them. That is not to say that a national education service containing, among other things some 25,000 schools, could be efficiently run directly from Whitehall. Some kind of regional, or local administration is needed for something as complex as a public education service. Whether or not those arrangements should contain some element of local democracy is open to debate. The important general point at issue is that the present situation is unstable and unsustainable.

There are three central duties in our public education service. First, is the duty vested in the Secretary of State to ensure that satisfactory provision is made for the education of the people of England and Wales. Second, is the duty, that is presently placed on LEAs, to ensure that sufficient and suitable school places are provided, and third, is the duty placed on parents to ensure that their children attend school, or are satisfactorily educated 'otherwise'. It is that second duty, to ensure the provision of sufficient and suitable places that is becoming increasingly problematical.

If the Government does not allow LEAs to influence schools significantly, it becomes increasingly nonsensical for the law to insist that the duty to ensure sufficient, suitable places lies with them. Almost equally anomalous are a number of other situations such as: the continuing role of LEAs as the employers of teachers while having little opportunity to influence what governors and schools do in relation to teaching staff and their employment; and the continued existence of local authority inspection and advisory services and a concern with quality assurance in the light of the Schools Act of 1992.

I could go on, but the point I want to make is that in our present situation it is the Government which is calling the tune and doing so in ways that make it clear that it no longer regards local education authorities as its major partner in a national system of education that is locally administered.

As for the schools they are all becoming increasingly autonomous. That is clearly true of those that opt for grant maintained status. But it is not very different for schools that are fully involved in LMS and whose governing bodies now have the power and influence conferred upon them by education law. Consequently, it is at the school level that most of the important decisions about priorities for local spending will be made. No doubt many of those decisions will be sensible and intelligent. But they are, in an important sense, self-interested decisions where the immediate concern is with what is of benefit to that particular institution.

That will lead, and has already led, to some marked improvements in efficiency and value for money at the school level. However, it is surely a triumph of hope over experience to expect that such self-interested, isolated, fragmented decisions, made in thousands of separate institutions, will add up to a sensible, effective and efficient national school system.

Already it is clear that some things of great value and high standards are suffering. Music, one of the undoubted gains in quality and standards in English education since the 1950s, is a case in point. That is because the gains in quality came, in the main, not from curricular music work in individual schools, but from the larger-than-school provision made by LEAs. It was that which was able to bring together and employ high quality instrumental music teachers; to provide centres where sufficiently large groups of young musicians could gather together to enable collective musicianship to be developed. It also made possible all kinds of ensemble and instrumental facilities, such as county youth and school symphony orchestras, jazz bands, choral groups, chamber groups and piano centres. You could no doubt add to music other fields of activity which, to be cost-effective *and* educationally effective, need to be organised, administered and conducted at a level over, above and beyond the individual school. The list would not be short. It would include such things as art and drama centres, remedial teaching support and teachers' centres of various kinds.

A national system of schooling, a proportion of which is compulsory, and which is free at point of delivery, can be governed and administered in a variety of different ways. It cannot, however, remain a public and equitable national service, compulsory for some part of its time, if it is to be shaped and determined by nothing other than the aggregation of the random, self-interested choices made by individuals in thousands of particular schools. A public education service must be subject to some degree of overall planning and organisation.

Of course, the balance between bureaucracy and direction on the one hand, and choice and enterprise on the other, is crucial – few dispute that. Some such balance there must be. It is the nature of it that is contested.

Currently the education service is undergoing enormous change, much of it necessary and required, and some of it undoubtedly beneficial. But it is not a requirement that such change, even when it involves fundamental modifications to received wisdom, should generate and actively sustain the degree of uncertainty and confusion that is prevalent in the system at the moment.

Given the Government's absolutely central position in all that is going on in education – a position it has quite purposely manoeuvred itself into – it is to the Government that we must look to give the lead in ending the confusion. A public education service not only requires some national and local organisation and planning if it is to be effective, efficient and equitable, it needs a vision; an underpinning philosophy. There must be some clarity about what the education service is for and where it is going. 'Where there is no vision the people perish.' (*Proverbs*)

Without such an overarching vision, the system risks becoming a stifling bureaucratic monster intent upon its own day-to-day survival in which people are treated like so much lost-property. Or, it becomes an anarchic free-for-all in which 'unto everyone that hath shall be given' and, even more worryingly, 'from him that hath not shall be taken away even that which he hath.'

There is, then, no clarity at present about the Government's vision for the public education service of this country. The notion of a free-market economy, allied with a narrow concentration on basic skills, that characterised some of the thinking of advisors to the early Thatcher Governments is still around and is reflected in some of what is now being enacted. It does not seem to have the drive and thrust it once enjoyed, to judge from recent Prime Ministerial and Government statements. Yet, ironically, the influence of right-wing think tanks on the Government's education thinking appears stronger under John Major than it was under Mrs Thatcher.

Vision and commitment are heady stuff and generate fierce argument. Nonetheless, all involved in education – teachers, parents and others more widely in the education service, employers and society at large – have a right to expect some explicit statement of vision from those who have put themselves in charge of the nation's destiny: some view about where it ought to be heading and what it should all add up to. Given such explicitness from our politicians we would be free to agree or disagree, or to press for amendments and changes of emphasis and direction. That is the democratic process.

We await The White Paper due in the next few days, I believe. No doubt we have our own differing hopes and fears about what it should contain. But I suspect, even allowing for our differences, we all want a White Paper that whatever else it does, sets out the Government's vision for the future direction, governance and management of the education service. We want that, not in any sense of cravenly waiting to be told what to do and believe. We want it because present circumstances make it imperative that the Government puts its cards on the table. If and when it does that, we can react as we feel fit. Sadly, I suspect we will have a long wait.

I suspect that if we were able to lift the veil hiding the Government's intentions for education we would find, not a coherent vision, worrying or otherwise, but uncertainty, confusion and incoherence.

The various education policies, consciously and unconsciously built into the ERA, have produced a situation where the intended and unintended instabilities of that legislation have brought the education service to the point where much of the old order is disintegrating. That is not necessarily a bad thing. But if – out of that disintegration of the old order – a better, more relevant, coherent, higher quality and equitable education service is to arise, the Government must say what it intends and take us, the people, into its confidence.

However, I suspect the Government might well have painted itself into a corner in which developing such an overarching vision is almost impossible. It has made it clear that it does not trust, or like, Local Education Authorities. Its vision will not, then, lead it to a new kind of partnership in education between central and local government. It has, in the recent past, shown equally strongly its suspicion of large-scale, non-accountable, unelected bureaucratic systems. Indeed, some of the shriller voices in the Government party have closely allied such bureaucracies with communism and left-wing socialism. That would seem to rule regional administrations out of court. Furthermore, it is clear to all non-partisan observers that simply letting the thousands of actors in the system take their own self-interested decisions, in the hope that they will add up to a coherent philosophy on which effective and efficient management and governance can be based, will not do either. There are not many alternatives left, and none that has any real credibility.

Consequently, it is difficult to gauge which way the Government will go in seeking to bring coherence and continuity to the education service – if, indeed, it seeks that at all. Without coherence and continuity, quality and standards of learning will not be raised.

The Government, and its immediate predecessors, have set in train a number of key and necessary changes in the education service in England and Wales. The present administration has raised the profile of the need to lift standards across the board: in particular the need to raise both our expectations and the achievements of pupils in the middle range of academic ability. It has recognised that it is with those pupils that our failure as a nation lies and that it is that failure that has most effect both on our performance as a nation and upon the quality of the adult life of many individuals. It has also, in its curricular and its assessment arrangements, started a process which tackles important issues concerned with what is to be studied by all pupils, its relevance to them and to the world in which they are growing up, as well as its importance to the health and wealth of the nation.

Give or take another decade or so, I believe we could have in place a sensible national curriculum and valid and manageable assessment arrangements. If that were so it would indeed be a great step forward.

There is also much promise of improved efficiency in the development of LMS and the greater autonomy that now exists at the individual school level. What is not clear yet, is whether or not there will be any feed-through from improved efficiency to higher standards and better quality. That is one of the many acts of faith embedded in the complex legislative structure of the ERA.

Perhaps most interesting, over the next year or so, is what will emerge from the new relationships being negotiated between governing bodies, head teachers and their senior staff, and the community served by the school. There are all kinds of possibilities for both good and ill, probably for both, and we will have to wait to see how they develop.

On the other hand, there is undoubtedly a lot of plain silliness emerging from the present legislative scene. There are worrying signs that the business of providing suitable and adequate school places, far from being eased and facilitated by recent legislation, is becoming more difficult and chaotic. To all involved in education with the wit and willingness to see, there are obvious limitations in a national, compulsory system of education on the freedom of choice that can be exercised by parents, pupils or schools. Indeed, it seems pretty clear that we could be heading for a state of affairs that, far from giving increased and improved choice of schools to parents, simply shifts the decision-making from LEAs to the individual school. If so, despite the Citizen's and Parent's Charters, schools will choose pupils; or rather, some schools will choose some pupils while others will have no choice at all.

Particularly saddening is the re-emergence of the search for a workable form of selection and segregation. Over the last thirty or forty years we have seen a fundamental shift in secondary education in this country from a selective system to one based mainly on comprehensive schools. In reality those schools do not present a monolithic, grey conformity, but are as varied and as different from each other as schools ever were. In fact, the old grammar schools were extremely similar; so much so that the HMI involved years ago in grammar school inspections could set down the curricular pattern and shape, and even the text books that would be in use, before ever reaching the school. There is no evidence that bears scrutiny which shows that standards of achievement at the end of secondary schooling have generally fallen.

Yet, through the pursuit of vouchers and selective systems we continually raise the notion of segregating pupils at an early age rather than concentrating our minds and energies on making the system we have work better. It is our besetting sin – the 'English sickness' in education.

In the international comparisons that have carried so much weight in the education debate in this country and abroad in recent years, we do as well as any other counry, and better than many, with regard to our most academically able pupils. We have about the same proportion as all other comparable countries of those who for one reason or another barely make a start in the educational process. Where we fail badly, in comparison with other developed countries, is with the broad range of ordinary pupils, the middle range and just below, of academic ability. We turn the vast majority of those out of our school system under-educated and under-qualified.

The English education system's greatest 'success' throughout its history, therefore, has been to fail most children. Our system is better than any other in the developed world at failing people, and turning them out from the education service with a sense that they have achieved nothing of any value. It is that issue above all others that we need to address if we are to raise the standards of education in this country and to have a decent, high quality and equitable education service. In tackling that issue, questions and debates about how to segregate pupils into academic and non-academic, vocational and non-vocational, practical and theoretical sheep and goats, at as early an age as fourteen, are not only irrelevant but downright counterproductive. Even worse is the call by the Prime Minister that we should return to a system of examining at the end of compulsory schooling that, by design, sets out to qualify only 25 per cent of pupils. No other comparable country does that.

International comparisons, though, are slippery things. There is nothing to be gained from trying simply to import the best of other countries' education systems. But there are lessons to be learned of the 'What does he know of England who only England knows?' kind. The message I would draw from my experience, over the years, of international comparisons is that all other developed countries keep a larger proportion of their pupils in a broad, general education for longer than we do. They qualify a much larger proportion of their pupils than we do in worthwhile ways, and the central drive of their education systems is to qualify the majority. They set out to do that without minimising the expectations of, and the standards achieved by, the most able and gifted. Every country somewhere has its Ivy League, or its *Grandes Ecoles*.

Yet here, sadly, in England there has re-emerged that old and wearyingly familiar voice from the right wing of the governing party, which claims that excellence can only be pursued in education at the expense of generally qualifying the majority; which sees a segregated and divided system as the only way of bringing about excellence; and which regards the only examinations worth having as being those that most people fail.

We began, back in the late 1970s and through to the ERA of 1988, to tackle that issue of failure in our system, through the GCSE and much of the national curriculum legislation and subsequent action. But beyond sixteen years of age we have not even begun to tackle it. The 'A' level, like a colossus, bestrides the sixteen to nineteen territory. Excellent as the 'A' level is at its best, the Government's determination to maintain it as a 'gold standard' is an unnecessary barrier to the work needed to bring together academic and vocational education, to provide a range of worthwhile routes beyond sixteen, through education and training. Just as the notion of a fixed, unchanging 'A' level is counterproductive, so is much that is emerging from the work of the National Council for Vocational Qualifications (NCVQ), which seems to be taking vocational education into ever narrower workplace competencies.

Any hope that an 'A' level that is now regarded as maintaining some kind of mythical academic 'gold standard', and vocational education that is disappearing into ever narrower workplace competencies, can come together to combine in a sensible post-sixteen pattern is forlorn. Nor will that coming together be aided by Diplomas and Higher Diplomas at the sixteen to nineteen stage: they seem little more than skimpy fig leaves vainly attempting to cover up the nakedness of what actually exists.

Nevertheless, there are reasons for hope and optimism as well as for concern and pessimism in the whirlwind of change and development affecting the education service. The Government needs to come out of the closet and assume the full the responsibilities of the position it has taken unto itself. In doing so it needs to act wisely. By that I do not mean that, in order to be wise, the Government should do what I think it must; rather, it needs to set out clearly what it wants to do and, in doing it, it needs the wisdom to begin to listen to the voices of all those with a legitimate interest in education. It is as damaging, and as nonsensical, to turn a deaf ear to the professionals in education as it is to believe that the professional is the only voice that should be heard. It is lacking in wisdom not to listen to the views of those long involved in administering and governing education at local level. It is shortsighted and ultimately counterproductive to believe, or appear to believe, that anybody who is not with us is against us.

Despite the undoubted strength and clearsightedness that can come from wiping away the ideological guff that settles, over time, like a thick accretion on services such as education, it is decidedly unwise to believe that altruism and disinterestedness are no longer important in education, or that they no longer exist and no longer fuel the actions and arguments of individuals.

In coming towards my conclusion I am reminded of a somewhat silly story. A man was taken by a friend of his, an employer, to see a brand new, hi-tech factory. They came to the heart of the works – a large, clean room in which, dotted about and apparently completely separated from each other, were various machines. The factory owner fed a piece of metal into the first and as they slowly walked through the room each of the machines, apparently unconnected, carried out its task on the metal. At the end, the last machine disgorged a completed object: a sort of metal tool. The factory owner turned to his friend and said, 'What do you think of that?' He replied, 'I can see that it works in practice, but does it work in theory?'

Without some underpinning theory, allied to a shared and generally accepted vision and philosophy, a public education service simply limps from one bureaucratic decision to another, or conversely, lurches around maniacally, subject to the whims and passions of self-interest and to the rantings of whichever fashionable voices are currently able to gain access to influential ears.

Sadly, despite the rhetoric of Citizen's and Parent's Charters, the Government shows little sign of being a listening Government.

When it does, it listens so selectively that most of those in the education service fear that what they have to say falls on deaf ears. The Government does not seem to listen to:

1. Heads and teachers; teacher associations; governors and education researchers, on the difficult issues of school effectiveness, value-added and league tables. It *does* listen to John Marks and the Adam Smith Institute.
2. Heads of schools; governing bodies; head teacher associations; vice-chancellors and teacher trainers, when it sets out to reform teacher training. It *does* listen to Sheila Lawlor whose critique of Initial Teacher Training is based on a somewhat selective reading of course prospectuses and is not complicated by ever having visited and systematically observed what goes on.
3. Public examination boards; chief examiners; most heads and teachers; HMI and large employers, when it sets out to squeeze the GCSE back into a GCE 'O' level mould. It *does* listen to the Centre for Policy Studies and a small group of independent school heads.
4. HMI; heads of effective primary schols, and non-ideologically driven experts, on the teaching of reading. It *does* listen to Martin Turner who initially claimed, on somewhat elusive evidence, that reading standards in England were falling across the board (not true) and that *the cause* was that primary schools had rushed, or been led, wholesale into modern, trendy teaching of reading based on the 'Real Books' approach (again, not true).

There is no crime in listening to your political friends. But a wise government listens more widely than that, and especially to those with no political axe to grind. It is not auspicious that the formal channels of advice about education to the Government appear to be either muzzled (e.g., HMI), or packed with people likely to say whatever the Government wants to hear (i.e., the NCC and SEAC).

In the 1940s Arthur Koestler, in a letter to a young airman, described how Turgenev used to set about writing. Apparently he sat at a table in a room of his house overlooking a busy main street. His feet were in a bowl of warm water; the curtains were half-drawn and the windows partly open. Koestler used that image to make a series of points about the business of writing. In particular he pointed out the need to be somewhat withdrawn from the day-to-day world, to be in touch with, but not wholly immersed in it – hence the half-drawn curtains and the partly open windows onto the main street. He also pointed out the need to draw on one's inner resources and not to stray too far away from them – the half-darkened room and feet in the bowl of warm water.

Essentially, Koestler shows that the good writer needs to be in the world, but not wholly of it. If Turgenev leans too far out of the window his feet come out of the bowl of water, and his ears are filled with the formless noise and babble of the crowd. If he closes the curtains and the windows, he ends up, sooner rather than later, describing nothing more than the wallpaper of the room and voices inside his own head, divorced from reality.

There is a risk in education that the Government is heading in the direction characterised by the writer in his closed, darkened room. It listens so selectively and has so firmly closed the windows and curtains that it does not seem to hear, or see, the education scene as most people out in the world experience it. In those circumstances it becomes all too easy to believe that the silence with which it has surrounded itself signifies contentment with the brave new world it is creating. The danger is that the reality may be more akin, as Tacitus put it long ago, to the Government 'making a wilderness and calling it peace'.

2

THE PECULIARITY OF THE ENGLISH

ANNE CORBETT

This chapter, which uses the most recent information available, evaluates England's educational provision in comparison with France, Germany and other European countries. It attempts an explanation of England's comparative backwardness in important areas, stresses the urgent need for radical advance in education and is designed to shake us out of a cultural defeatism.

Anne Corbett is a distinguished educational journalist. She writes regularly for the Times Educational Supplement *on education in France and Europe as a whole. She also teaches on an international relations course at the Université Paris I – Panthéon-Sorbonne.*

INTRODUCTION

The word Europe appears only once in the White Paper, *Choice and Diversity*: 'The transformation of education we have undertaken is designed to ensure that our education system becomes the best in Europe.' The document's sixty-four pages, prelude to the sixteenth item of Conservative education legislation since 1979 (now going through Parliament), have just one other reference to the world beyond British shores: 'We intend to create a stable system of education that sets international levels of excellence. Other leading nations have high standards and a high degree of specialisation. We can outstrip them.'

In the Government's eyes: 'This requires not only a new framework but also renewed commitment from parents, staff and pupils. The framework is being established and the commitment already exists. We are creating the conditions necessary to harness that commitment and raise standards to new levels.'

This is the proposed new framework for schools, designed for the surely common European century almost on us. Even if one ignores the paragraph's internal inconsistencies about the need for a 'new commitment' by parents, staff and pupils, and the fact that the new commitment 'already exists', the tone is embattled and unreasoned.

One aim of this chapter is to demonstrate that it is cruel, if not irresponsible, to adopt a bravado tone – 'we can outstrip them' – and to refuse to define what is 'the best'. Educational policy marks a generation at a time.

Another is to suggest that the Government's proposals, far from being 'new', all look suspiciously familiar. Much of what they are proposing with the philosophy of 'choice and diversity' and scope for individual initiative is driving a well-known wedge between the strong and the weak. Take just one example of the perverse effects as underlined in recent news stories. Money is being poured by some schools into the employment of PR consultants, whom one might think of as fulfilling a fringe activity. Others are being forced to sack experienced teachers, who by every definition must be the school's most valuable resource. And why? Because teachers at the top of the salary scale are a heavy item in individually managed budgets.

A third aim is to show why current policy is particularly inappropriate in a context which is epitomised by the Single European Act, on the one hand, and a consensus about the knowledge input to economic growth, on the other. Nations – and international companies – now compete for skills in the way they used to compete for trade.

The Government's approach may not be surprising. The White Paper's proposals are consistent with a 'peculiarity' of the English political system, first discerned in the nineteenth century in which the state acts as a policeman but does little to empower. But today such a strategy is not only inappropriate; it is, for many of Britain's young, a tragedy on a scale which ought to shake some of their elders out of the defeatism that nothing culturally ingrained can change.

In that context there is a great phrase from the 1940s which comes from the Frenchman Jean Monnet. At the time he was a civil servant struggling with the seemingly intractable problem of finding a strategy which would enable France's enfeebled coal and steel industry to compete with their German rivals, who had the opportunity to build anew. 'When you are blocked by facts you need to change the framework in which you put them,' he said. And he did not do badly. Out of his cogitations came the first draft for the EEC, in the form of the European Coal and Steel Community. I am asking – and it is my fourth aim – that we too register the wider context, given that we seem blocked on a national one.

IN AN INTERNATIONAL LEAGUE TABLE

This is not to say that, in its educational policy, the British Government has refused to adapt to international trends. After the Second World War, the governments of all the developed nations restructured systems which had provided elementary education for the masses and secondary education for an elite. In the 1960s they pushed the general expansion into the hitherto sacred domains of the universities and other institutions of higher education. The 1973 oil price rise made all start to reconsider the wisdom of a policy widely held to be based on quantity rather than on quality. James Callaghan's Ruskin speech in 1976 was the first stone to be cast into a British pool of concern about making education more cost effective (Moon, 1990). Recent policies for a national curriculum and the concern with evaluation – whether by inspection, tests or league tables – are very much part of the trend.

But if we take recent comments which draw on an international perspective, then the Government in Britain, or rather England and Wales, has chosen a peculiar way. Take Sir Claus Moser, who made the celebrated speech a couple of years ago claiming that the majority of British pupils were not receiving an education worthy of 'a civilised nation'. It was his speeches and the public response which led the Hamlyn Foundation to fill a gap consciously ignored by the Government and to finance a National Commission on Education.

Or take Eric Bolton, former Chief Inspector of Schools (see the preceding chapter), who has also attracted much attention from the public: he picks out the British failure to do well by the broad mass of pupils. 'We turn most of those out of our school system under-educated and under-qualified,' in comparison with other countries. He too blames a segregationist, peculiarly 'English sickness' which 'succeeds' by imposing selective processes under which most children fail.

Howard Davies, Director General of the CBI, prefaces his critique of the White Paper with a reference to the World Education Forum ranking the UK 'a worrying twenty out of twenty-two on the ability of the education system to meet the needs of international competition in the 1990s'.

Recent remarks from the private sector's preparatory schools' association may, in comparison, seem almost archaic in their choice of example – that Britain's neglect of training lower and middle management will mean in a free movement Europe that Britons are left doing menial jobs, like those for 'waiters, porters and lavatory attendants'.

But you have in those four examples pointers to three elements which are generally agreed to encompass the aims of an education system, and which have indeed been summarised as such by the National Commission on Education. First, an educational system ought to be trying to provide entitlement and opportunity to all individuals. Second, it must transmit knowledge and society's cultural values. Third, it should provide the workforce (and thus the nation) with knowledge and competence for a competitive world.

In those terms the White Paper's approach is either inadequate or vicious. In his foreword, the Prime Minister John Major pays lip service to education as the birthright of every child: 'The Government are determined that every child in this country should have the very best start in life . . . Education can make or mar each child's prospects. Each has but one chance in life.' There is not, however, a commitment to universal pre-school education, which has been known for years to have beneficial effects, and has been taken up by other countries (Pugh, 1992).

Then, once you leave aside the national curriculum, the Government's imperatives for the nation in the 1990s are three of a particular kind: a moral mission – setting a framework for 'going to school, staying there and learning', strengthening a (Christian) moral dimension, and giving schools strong leadership; a money-saving purpose – weeding out surplus places; and an ideologically segregationist agenda – relying on 'parent-driven selection' to create the higher standards desired.

No one would deny that it is an essential task of the school to inculcate the values which strengthen a society, though no doubt disagreeing with some of the terms put forward here, they are not normally the only ones. But the Government finishes there, with a flourish of demagogy and partisan politics. Its 'vision' as proclaimed in the White Paper, is centred on a rich array of schools and colleges, all teaching the national curriculum and playing to their strengths, allowing parents to choose the schools best suited to their children's needs, and all enjoying parity of esteem ... Talent is not uniform. Our education system cannot afford to be uniform either. We will have an education system that meets the needs of our children – not one in which children are, for example, forced to conform to the needs of some theoretically-based undifferentiated and under-performing system.

There is no mention of 'human resources'. Yet much of the world has moved beyond a belief in monetarism and the dominance of the business cycle as the recipe for economic growth. One only has to look at the projects backed by such culturally different organisations as the EC and OECD.

But significantly these organisations are not going back to the demand cycle theory inspired by Keynes. What they have become interested in is the supply side – education, investment, research and development, trade reform, intellectual property rights and so on (Barro *et al.*, 1992). In other words, they are saying education pays.

Though this might have been obvious to generations of teachers, it is thanks to economists that education now has this international resonance. For it is research economists who have shaken the neo-classical theory of growth which sees the output of an economy as dependent on the amount of capital and labour employed. Their studies of growth in various countries suggested that this could not be so. Otherwise why should decades of heavy investment in India have yielded so little, and in South Korea and Taiwan so much? Much of the difference between them lay, it was suggested, in the very different levels of education of their population, and their receptivity to new ideas.

In recent years this work has been followed up to produce a general theory of 'human capital': that it is the lack of investment in human resources, not lack of investment in physical capital, which keeps poor countries from catching up – or allows others to slip. In a global economy, the only chance of prosperity for high wage, advanced economies is to have a workforce which is cleverer and more flexible than those in low-wage economies, and which is thus able to produce goods better and more quickly. This applies not only to management but also to the core of the labour force, for the automation revolution, too, needs competent people to manage it.

A number of recent studies show Britain in danger of paying the price of sticking to its 'peculiarity' and being one 'theory revolution' too late. For while it has been a constant of international comparisons that the cleverest in the British system can take on all comers, it has been shown time and again that Britain does badly by the broad majority.

One famous study several years ago showed young British workers taking two years to learn what young German workers learnt in two months (Steedman and Wagner, 1989). Two studies for the National Commission sound other alarm bells (Raffe, 1992; Finegold, 1992). One analyses the argument put up by the Government and others to suggest that the exceptionally high British drop-out rate from education at sixteen is not as bad as it seems since most go into part-time further education. The study suggests that, on the contrary, given the current basis of further education, this is in fact a disaster. The other study produces troubling evidence of the low skills equilibrium the British have allowed to develop.

There is a further critique developing from the recent OECD report on indicators of educational performance in OECD member countries in 1988 (1992). When it appeared in September 1992, the press in OECD's twenty-two member states naturally constructed national league tables. Britain comes out reasonably in the most general comparisons. It is around average on the proportion of GDP allocated to education; the level of education of the population in general (aged twenty-four to sixty-five) comes out better than some obvious rivals like France.

But on closer examination Britain comes out well below average in some strategic areas, including two already mentioned: nursery education and the education of the sixteen-to-eighteen-year-olds. It also spends less *per capita* on school pupils in the public system than most countries. On the other hand, it spends much more and does much better in its system of university education, with an impressive 94 per cent success rate.

The originality of the OECD report is that it enables one, for the first time in international educational comparisons, to relate certain aspects of educational performance to each country's social and economic factors and, in broad-brush terms, its organisational style.

How, in that light, does the Government's claim to know how to construct 'the best' system stand up? The answer is that such a claim is ridiculous. The OECD work exposes British demagogy (and, to be fair, foreign demagogy too, no doubt). For what it shows is that there is no single model of success. There is no 'best' system of management, no 'best buy' to be added to a hypothetical education shopping list.

Wide variations in performance are a feature of centralised systems, decentralised systems and such parent influenced systems as the USA's: there is no definitive answer on success rates in selective and non-selective secondary systems; performances are subject to a wide variation in both. There is no single best location geographically: northern Europe does not do better everywhere than the countries of the Mediterranean – for example, Spain now produces more graduates per head of the age group than Britain.

These results should be encouraging for those who want to challenge the Government on its education policy. They are proof that there is nothing mechanistic about the way education systems operate.

For what also emerges is the nature of each country's political – or politico-historical – choices and the very widely varying education systems which they have produced.

In this light, British results can be compared with those of a similar sized but historically different country, like France. France actually spends less of its GDP on education than Britain, but it has a far higher proportion of the age group in pre-school education. It encourages a high general level of secondary education for all. And it has an exceptional proportion of science and engineering graduates which, like Japan and Germany, it defines as its elite (UK figures were not available).

However, France treats its university education system miserably badly in financial terms and only 55 per cent of its original entrants appear to get a degree. But where Britain was letting in only 10 per cent of its age group at the time, France lets in over 18 per cent, many of whom use the open access university as a stepping stone to other studies.

In other words, judgements need to be tempered depending on what is being measured. British universities' 94 per cent success rate is an undoubted tribute to the institutions, but it is not a flattering measure of opportunity for the age group. Nor, combined with Britain's relatively poor secondary education figures, does it suggest Britain is necessarily doing well by society as a whole.

In France, where rhetorical commitments are constantly directed towards the meritocratic individual and the nation's needs, the pattern is very different. The French do provide a good educationl start for almost everyone. There is a high general level of education taking in almost all up to the age of eighteen, and it takes evident care of its scientific elite. But it has left a population at university level to look after itself (supported by family or work), on the grounds that it is motivated and that what it most needs is an open door.

Here, then, is more evidence for those who wish to argue that the British system is too 'consumer' driven. It is only too easy to see that other systems do set their aims differently.

HISTORY REPEATING ITSELF?

In fact, it is becoming fashionable from all parts of the political spectrum to see Britain as a prisoner of its nineteenth-century past – sections of the right, which simply used to berate a 1960s left for its 'egalitarian' policies, now join in. To take some recent comment on the subject, *The Economist* (21 November 1992) also puts Britain's system in an international context, concluding: 'It would be hard to imagine an educational system more likely to hold up economic growth than one which was designed by anti-industrial snobs in the mid-nineteenth century and then redesigned by anti-industrial egalitarians a century later.'

But for those specifically interested in the history of education, Brian Simon's four-volume work (1960-91) offers a much more comprehensive explanation of the evolution of British education than is contained in this sweeping assertion. Here is evidence of the power of class which enabled England to develop an entirely segregated system of education for the governing class in the mid-nineteenth century, 'one that has no parallels in any other country'. Here too – and Simon has been a pioneer – is evidence of how deeply the British have continued to integrate a segregationist philosophy. In the 1930s the country was also unique in its attachment to the doubtful 'science' of 'psychometry' and intelligence testing. Now it is unique in being so fixed to a free market philosophy in public education.

It is significant that the military historian Correlli Barnett (1986), who is unlikely to share Simon's left wing views, is equally indignant. Seeking to explain Britain's industrial decline since the Second World War, he rages in a properly military way at Britain's 'half cock' education and training for continually failing to exploit the talents of a very large part of the population. Underneath the victory bunting in 1945 was a nation in a position of 'crushing inferiority' in relation to the Germans.

Barnett concludes his book bitterly and provocatively by quoting Sir Geoffrey Holland, then director of the Manpower Services Commission, but who (from January 1993) becomes the new permanent secretary to the Department for Education. Holland had this to say on Britain's backwardness in education for industrial capability compared with her rivals: 'We're not only not in the same league, we're not in the same ball game.'

Yet it is not for lack of trying by private citizens and official bodies to push the country on a different course. For a hundred years prior to the Second World War, numerous bodies had attempted to convince public opinion and governments that Britain's battles were already being lost in the nation's schools and universities. In 1861 the Royal Commission on the State of Popular Education – at a time when education was not compulsory – was appalled to find that few of those who did not go to school ever learnt to read (cf. Maclure, 1975). The Royal Commission on the Public Schools of 1864 found the education of the upper classes to be narrower than it had been three centuries earlier and natural science teaching 'practically excluded'. In 1868 another Royal Commission warned that the 'industrial classes' did not have the basis of a 'sound general education on which alone technical education can rest' and without which 'our undeniable superiority in wealth and perhaps in energy will not save us from decline.' And so on.

These commissions had done their homework. They reported what was happening overseas – the importance the continentals attached to science teaching and high level engineering training; the recognition they gave to the fact that the 'industrial classes' who represented the nation's principal reservoir of ability needed educating too. But British governments, rich on the profits of Empire, chose not to listen to advice on educational policy from specialists and public figures.

This historical perspective on English peculiarities raises another point which concerns an ingrained cultural attitude to the role of the state. This thinking emerged from a tradition the present Government will refuse to recognise: that of the Marxist New Left, stimulated by a 1964 essay by Perry Anderson. But this debate has been so widely joined that it is no longer of merely sectarian interest. The subject was the explanation for the apparent failure of (English-dominated) British governments to achieve modernisation through the instrument of the state, as has occurred successfully in countries as different as France, Sweden and Japan.

Some of the arguments may seem esoteric but it joins directly with our concern: was this failure inherent in the fact that Britain's land-owning aristocracy, unlike that of its continental neighbours in the nineteenth century, successfully absorbed its bourgeoisie and thereby stifled an entrepreneurial class? (Anderson, 1992; Thompson, 1978) Was it the English hegemony of the UK? (Nairn, 1981) Or was the prime reason the fact that Britain was the first industrialised nation? Having accomplished this under a nineteenth-century liberal regime it saw no reason to modernise (Hobsbawm, 1968).

While all these lines of thought may play a part, the debate has been crucially enriched for our argument by the insistence of David Marquand (1988) on the pervasive social and political effects of early nineteenth-century liberalism on the creation of uniquely English attitudes to the state: 'the values and assumptions of (Britain's) elites, the doctrines disseminated by her universities and newspapers, the attitudes and patterns of behaviour of her entrepreneurs and workers were stamped indelibly by this experience.'

One consequence, taken up by those pushing for constitutional reform, is that parliamentary success in making the British monarchy constitutional tends to make the British population unconcerned with what should be considered their rights. The English have a political culture with a particular conception of freedom which is anti-absolutist rather than democratic.

A further important contribution comes from Andy Green (1990). His comparative study of the formation of the state education systems of England, France, Prussia and the USA, shows up another English distinction. Unlike the USA or France or Prussia, mid nineteenth-century British governments were never forced to see in education an instrument of cultural unity or a pillar of democracy. The British already had a relatively rich and peaceful society. They neutralised Chartism and certainly never faced revolution. Governments were able to develop a national system piecemeal, which in essence remained dependent on voluntary bodies and, overwhelmingly, the Church. There was no power group behind the critics, particularly those who said the country would be better off if it paid more attention to the formation of the intellect and less to moral training, following the continental example.

The essential message comes through loud and clear: Britain's apparently archaic political culture is still strong. So we should not be surprised that a 1990s government can still put forward a strategy based on early nineteenth-century ideas which amount to an old-fashioned liberalism. For the forty-four new powers which the Secretary of State will acquire under the proposed legislation are essentially policing functions. The framework of choice which the legislation will put in place is not an educational philosophy.

Those who speak of John Patten as using the language of Adam Smith and wielding the baton of Napoleon have got it wrong. Napoleon *did* have an educational vision.

OR A DIFFERENT FUTURE?

It is devastating to follow the British education debate from outside Britain, and watch the derision with which the Government regards specialist knowledge, its attacks on an educational 'establishment', seeing the public interest as of no concern. This is bad enough in the popular press, but it is truly shocking in the Government. The White Paper contains one particularly stunning example of the way the Government ignores the checks and balances inherent in the administration of public institutions: it refers to elected education committees as 'obstacles' in the way of organisational flexibility.

But just as the studies of education in the nineteenth century have illustrated a public fatalism about what governments chose to do (or not do) so it seems obvious today that nothing much will happen to deter the Government from its tack without a major cultural shift.

The question is whether 'Europe' provides that shift. Without a doubt the Community's various aspects already condition directly or indirectly many aspects of people's daily lives. There is a strong case for saying that it has become a frame of reference – both a warning and an inspiration. The march of time, as much as treaty texts, is shaking much of Britain out of its insularity.

Signs of it are visible among the business community. A revived CBI is campaigning hard – with the logic and rhetoric of 'human capital' – for partnership with the education community, the recognition that learning needs to be lifelong and that it needs to build on competence as well as knowledge and skills.

There are signs of it within the institutions of government and in the representative organisations which all need to be well informed. The Brussels link to the other eleven member states provides permanent education for many, from civil servants to the representatives of teachers' and employers' organisations, and the pressure groups.

At the same time there is a 'citizen's Europe' which is becoming entrenched. In the education world this is pronounced. British students may not be as enthusiastic and as knowledgeable about the EC as their French equivalents who voted 80 per cent in its favour in the Maastricht referendum. But they are assiduous in exploiting the networks of programmes like ERASMUS which provides top-up grants for university exchange students, and PETRA, its further education equivalent. Dozens of universities, and hundreds, if not thousands, of schools now have their 'Eurolink'. International partnerships are the *sine qua non* of much research.

As teachers regularly point out (Austin, 1992), much of this is done despite the barriers to easy contact that exist, rather than because they have been lowered. They naturally complain that there is no comprehensive system of credit accumulation and transfer in further education operating across the UK's borders, though it is clear that more and more might like to think European as they see jobs in Britain melt away. Or that there is not a more European dimension in the curriculum.

For many 'Europe' has brought new ideas and new friendships and the possibility of new and different work at a multitude of levels. But there are two major exceptions and one of the exceptions has numbers and the other exception has power. On every EC-wide poll the British come out as the most hostile and the most ill-informed about Community institutions. As measured by the EC's own polls, public opinion in November 1992 in most EC countries was between 53 and 63 per cent in favour of proposals for closer political and economic union. It was only in Germany and Denmark that governments did not appear to have a clear majority of public opinion on their side, and even there it was far above the British level.

In November 1992 a Eurobarometer poll showed that only 25 per cent of the British said they would support the Maastricht proposals. Though they are not of course being allowed to vote, one can read into this context a dire warning from the highly marginal French referendum: Europe has the potential to split an entire society. In France the significant divisions on the vote on Europe were not the institutionally contained in a left *versus* right divide. They were largely sociological. Much of the 'No' vote came from the marginalised – the unemployed, the agricultural workers on the rampage, and those in unskilled jobs. Though some leading French politicians did their country a service in helping (in a pro-'Yes' climate) to make opposition respectable, the clarity of the divisions were striking; enough to sharpen the French government's continuing concern about the population at large – and about those students and pupils, in particular, who do not have the skills to flourish in the single market.

Then there is the second British exception: the British Government, which despite its activity in trade and industry and in finance, avoids any concept of Europe as a structural element in society. This is all of a piece with its aversion to planning for the long term, and its perverse ambiguity about an educational philosophy.

As I was finishing this paper I came across a lecture by Alastair Morton, chief executive of Eurotunnel and pillar of British industry. He now knows a great deal about engineering worldwide. He was bemoaning the break-up of British expertise and engineering excellence. Its cause, he said, was 'the destructive influence' of short-term market forces. He feared for the inability of the great firms to get in on the next stage – the 'very major projects which spring up in Greater Europe over the next decade – tunnels under the Alps, bridges over the Baltic, cities adapted for high speed rail'. And he had this warning:

> Will we in Britain lead the way? It seems unlikely. At the end of the day it is the matching of . . . management . . . capital and the crucially important role of government in long-term development of the domestic economy. If your home rulers don't have a clue how to harness capital and management to . . . programmes, you soon lose the capacity to tackle big projects. You become disconnected from the international scene. You become peripheral. (Morton, 1992)

This does not seem so distant from the concerns expressed here. The education of the nation is a very big project too. Have the home rulers a clue?

REFERENCES

P. Anderson, *English Questions*, Verso, London 1992.
M. Austin, *Times Educational Supplement*, 6 November 1992.
C. Barnett, *The Audit of War*, Macmillan, London 1986.
R. Barro *et al.*, 'Economic Growth: Explaining the Mystery, a Description of the Work of Paul Romer', in *The Economist*, 4 January 1992.
D. Finegold, 'Breaking Out of the Low Skills Equilibrium', NCE Briefing no.5, July 1992.
A. Green, *Education and State Formation*, Macmillan, London 1990.
E. Hobsbawm, *Industry and Empire*, Weidenfeld and Nicholson, London 1968.

S. Maclure, *Educational Documents, England and Wales, 1816 to the Present*, Chapman and Hall, London 1975.

D. Marquand, *The Unprincipled Society*, Cape, London 1988.

B. Moon, 'Patterns of Control: Reforming West European Schools, *British Journal of Sociology*, vol.41, no.3, September 1990.

A. Morton, Speech to Institution of Structural Engineers, October 1992.

T. Nairn, *The Break Up of Britain*, NLB/Verso, London 1981.

OECD, *Education at a Glance*, Paris 1992 (available from HMSO, London).

G. Pugh, *Times Educational Supplement*, 13 November 1992.

D. Raffe, 'Participation of Sixteen- to Eighteen-Year-Olds in Education and Training', NCE Briefing no.3, May 1992.

B. Simon, *Studies in the History of Education*, in four vols, Lawrence & Wishart, London 1960-91.

H. Steedman and K. Wagner, 'Productivity, machinery and skills: clothing manufacture in Britain and Germany', *National Institute Economic Review*, May 1989.

E.P. Thompson, 'The Peculiarities of the English', in *The Poverty of Theory and Other Essays*, Merlin Press, London 1978.

3

POLICY-MAKING AND THE USE AND MISUSE OF EVIDENCE

CAROLINE V. GIPPS

Caroline Gipps is Reader in Education at the Institute of Education, University of London, where she specialises in primary education, particularly in issues of assessment. This is an abridged version of her presidential address to the British Education Research Association, delivered at its annual conference at the University of Stirling in August 1992. The complete version of this address appears in **British Educational Research Journal**, *Vol. 19, No. 1, 1993.*

In the summer of 1991 seven-year-olds sat the Standard Assessment Tasks (SATs) as part of national assessment for the first time. The reporting and publicity over those results gave rise to two of the most shameful and unsavoury events in recent years. First, Kenneth Clarke, the then Secretary of State for Education, announced in an article published in a Sunday tabloid, four days before the results were officially available, that the figures would show that nearly a third of seven-year-olds were unable to recognise three letters of the alphabet (*Mail on Sunday*, 15 December 1991). This information was then repeated the same day on the BBC's 'The World This Weekend' radio programme and in many other media slots. In fact, the figures showed that less than 2.5 per cent of the seven-year-olds tested were at this level of competence. Mr Clarke's 28 per cent of seven-year-olds were actually those who had not reached Level Two in reading, whereas his comments implied that they had not reached Level One. Whether witting or unwitting, this error set up in the public's mind that something is terribly amiss not only in the teaching of reading, but in primary education in general. As we know no amount of retraction or apology could make the same impact as the initial claims – indeed there was none. The National Association for the Teaching of English (NATE) eventually received a written apology from BBC Chairman Marmaduke Hussey who said that it was too late to offer a correction (*TES*, 24 April 1992, BBC Apologises for Reading Story Error) and suggested they write a letter to Feedback, the Radio 4 programme which deals with complaints.

Next, the results for seven-year-olds were put into LEA league tables (DES, 1991) and published, despite schools and LEAs having been informed that, since it was technically a trial run, no such thing would happen, *and* despite evidence from an independent evaluation commissioned at Leeds University by SEAC that the national assessment data were undependable. The final draft of the Leeds report was received at SEAC on 9 December, two weeks before the LEA league tables were published. That the report had not yet been approved by SEAC and that it had not been passed on to the Minister is not really in doubt, but one would expect, in a system which was concerned with efficiency and interested in facts and accuracy for such information (even in draft status), action to halt the league tables. Far from it; and the LEAs at the bottom of the league table were pilloried, while Clarke went on to blame poor teaching and Labour-led councils' high spending and inefficiency (*Guardian* 7 April 1992, 'Heat on Thatcher Aide Tests Furore'). In fact the Leeds draft report (finally published in the last week of July 1992) stating that the results were unreliable had added:

> In a context where the results of assessment may be made public, schools with large numbers of ethnic minority children, children from deprived social backgrounds or even younger rather than older children, would not appear in a particularly good light. The reasons for this would under these circumstances have little to do with the quality and appropriateness of the education being offered.

This would appear to be either gross incompetence on behalf of Mr Clarke's professional advisers, or political handling of unpalatable evidence. As with the misinformation on the Reading SATs, the delay over publication meant that the information about unreliability came too late for the LEAs at the bottom of the league tables and had a profound effect on public opinion.

As an example of the discourse of derision we have Education

Ministers Tim Eggar and Michael Fallon attacking the work of Harvey Goldstein and Desmond Nuttall which has consistently criticised the use of raw data to evaluate schools. Eggar said, 'we must not cover up underachievement with fiddled figures' (*TES*, 22 November 1991, ' "Fiddled" Figures Scorned'). Kenneth Clarke referred to them as 'Nutstein and Goldall', 'pretending' he had never heard of them or their work; Fallon said, 'we will not be dressing up the facts, obscuring the real level of performance by altering outcomes to take account of spurious measures of disadvantage or deprivation.' It took the Headmistress of Cheltenham Ladies College to retort that this was an 'arrogant and ignorant' response (*Evening Standard*, 6 November 1991, 'Fallon Snubs Professors' Exam Plea'). The independent sector of course knows only too well that there is a very high correlation between the level of academic selectivity of a school and its academic success. As the Head of probably the most academically selective boys' public school, Westminster, commented on a league table of independent schools, 'I wonder if you realise what a disservice you do to so many schools by concocting a league table of this kind?' (*Daily Telegraph*, 5 September 1991, 'More Schools Aspire to the Top Table').

Probably the most ill-informed comment on an educational issue, with a direct throwback to the reported seven-year-old SAT results, came from Mr Alan Amos, MP who is concerned about the amount of play activity in nursery schools – 'Mr Amos believes there is too much project work in nursery schools and that there should be more teaching of the class as a whole.' He said the poor results of seven-year-olds in reading and maths demonstrated the need to monitor what went on in the early years. (*TES*, 13 December 1991, 'Checks on Nursery Schools'). At this point it is worth remembering that Mr Fallon said he liked the Report on Primary Education by Alexander, Rose and Woodhead because it was refreshingly free of ideology! (*TES*, 8 November 1991, 'Streaming "May Begin at Nine" ').

For developments in policy that are 'refreshingly free' of educational support one must cite the reduction in coursework in GCSE. Despite early problems over organisation and timing, it is clear to many parents, teachers and HMI, that coursework encourages pupils to keep working through the year, and requires coverage of a wider part of the syllabus rather than 'topic-spotting' for an exam (HMI, 1988). It enables pupils to be assessed on a wider range of tasks than do traditional exams, and allows a broader range of candidates the opportunity to show what they can do. What is more, the traditional pencil and paper exam cannot test the whole of the national curriculum.

Not to labour the point, 'A' and 'AS' levels and modular courses are to follow the same pattern with reduced coursework and a terminal exam (even for modular courses) which will effectively reduce the advantages of modular study and limit the possibility of 'A' and 'AS' levels being brought closer to vocational courses. This move even flies in the face of the employers, given the recommendations of the CBI in their report 'Towards a Skills Revolution' for more varied teaching and assessing methods in all post-sixteen courses (*TES*, 10 January 1992, ' 'A' Level Limits Will Hamper Reform').

All in all, this looks like regression flying in the face of 'expert' opinion, that now derided commodity. What lies behind it is the belief from the right, particularly the Centre for Policy Studies, that the only appropriate form for high status examinations is the one we have had in the past (*TES*, 10 January 1992, 'Think Tank Cuts Back in Coursework') in that 'golden age' we all remember when education served us so well – the terminal unseen examination. The other problem seems to be that more pupils are gaining GCSEs than was the case in the old days of 'O' level and CSE. (This, of course, was one of the intentions of GCSE.) This has been interpreted as meaning that standards must be falling and Mr Clarke's fear 'seems to be that people *who don't deserve* it are getting qualifications, staying on at school' (*TES*, 29 November 1991).

If any further example were needed that we have lost our way it is the apparent disregard for the group of children who are difficult to educate, or who come to school with few advantages (and who might expect schooling to support them). In the world of LMS, selection, grant maintained schools and league tables, such children, particularly those with special needs, are fairly unmarketable commodities. As the Director of the National Children's Bureau put it, current policies 'appeal to the constituency of achieving parents, essentially a group quite capable of looking after themselves' (*TES*, 17 January 1992, 'Needy Child Must Not be Abandoned'). Those of us who warned about the social implications of the 1988 Education Act (Gipps, 1990) with its combination of LMS, published national assessment results, and emphasis on competition (which would effectively overwhelm the advantages of a common entitlement curriculum) were castigated as overly negative and as harbingers of doom. It gives little pleasure to see that, item by item, we are being proved right – from the rise in the number of exclusions, to the increase in children going to *separate* SEN provision, to the emptiness of the rhetoric of parental choice for all.

A fair competition, after all, is one in which the best person wins (not one in which everyone has the chance to gain something) and free choice for some is the loss of choice for others. What sort of soul is our generation passing on to the next?

As is becoming increasingly clear, the concept of market choice allows the articulate middle and educated classes to exert their privilege (whilst not appearing to). Both the market and the chooser operate in terms of self-interest, and the result is exclusion and differentiation, rather than freedom and choice. Choice is not to be confused with selection. How the system copes with unchosen schools and unselected children is likely to be a major dilemma. Chubb and Moe, Americans who were invited to analyse the British system write this dilemma off in two paragraphs, which completely underestimates the task.

> The standard criticisms of choice are aimed at the free market. They argue that people are not well enough informed to make good choices, that people lack transportation to the schools they prefer, that schools will discriminate in admissions, that private schools will prosper at the expense of state schools, and so on. And because these problems primarily affect the poor and minorities, they say, a choice system would push these people into second-class schools, while the economically advantaged would behave like bandits.
>
> Choice is not a free market system. Its 'educational markets' operate within an institutional framework, and the government's job is to design the framework so that these concerns are dealt with. (*Sunday Times Magazine*, 9 February 1992, 'The Classroom Revolution')

We have, of course, heard very little of this 'framework'. This is all a far cry from Dewey:

> What the best and wisest parent wants for his own child, that must the community want for all its children. Any other ideal for our schools is narrow and unlovely; acted upon, it destroys are democracy . . . Only by being true to the full growth of all the individuals who make it up, can society by any chance be true to itself. (Dewey, 1915, p7)

HOW DID WE GET WHERE WE ARE?

I shall now refer to a letter from Sir Douglas Black (the Chief Medical Officer) (*Guardian*, 9 March 1992) about the health care system, but it could equally be about education.

I have just got back from a conference in New York on health care associated with social deprivation. We may have our problems in this country, but the Americans, as is customary, have far bigger ones. And all this, in spite of the most expensive health care in the world. Two years ago in the *Guardian* I asked, why should we be seeking to imitate the American system? The question remains unanswered.

It is my belief that until they adopt, and we restore, a health care system grounded in equity, and not one which allows market forces to dictate a shallow entrepreneurism, health problems will not be tackled in the most economic and efficient way. Good health care cannot be achieved for the rich or the poor, unless there is good health care for all.

I include this because we need to remember that the shift in policy-making, away from one based on discussion and evidence is not only happening in education. As Jonathan Rosenhead, Professor of Operational Research at the LSE, points out (*Guardian*, 5 May 1992, 'Platform: Politics of the Gut Reaction'), the demise of the Central Policy Review Staff – the original 'Think Tank' – set up by Edward Heath, and its eventual replacement by the Policy Unit, the Centre for Policy Studies and the Adam Smith Institute, marked a shift from policy choice based on evidence and argument to one based on principles and gut reaction. Rosenhead describes what he calls the impoverished policy process in which the think tanks promote policy through strong value assertions and then proceed directly to detailed prescriptions. Argumentation is intuitive; there is appeal at most to anecdotal evidence but not to research. As examples of the result of this abbreviated policy process with slipshod or absent analysis he cites: the NHS reforms, the poll tax, opting out for schools and the student loans 'fiasco'. Rosenhead places at the root of this movement an ideology with a semi-mystical belief in the beneficial properties of market forces and a disbelief in the power of reason; this has resulted, he concludes, in a 'wilful failure to concede a significant role to reason in the practice of collective decision-making'.

Anthony Sampson, revisiting the *Anatomy of Britain* in 1992 (*Independent on Sunday*, 29 March 1992) just before the 1992 election charted the growing centralisation of power and the loss of voice for those out of power:

Since the seventies, the national cast of public characters has narrowed strikingly. The earlier drama included a range of major speaking parts, including trades unionists, local councillors, vice-chancellors, scientists, regional leaders and maverick politicians. Now the story line and supporting characters have been pared down to the central plot, revolving around money, the Treasury and – above all – Downing Street.

John Major inherited a much more centralised system than it had been a decade earlier, dominated by personality and financial controls. The character of government has also become more uniform in its exclusion of questioning and dissent. Sampson concludes that the last thirteen years have seen the British power structure concentrated at the top, while representation of people further down has become weaker through the undermining of local government, regional powers and trade unions. This erosion of democracy is accompanied by a growing underclass of families disconnected from the system and out of reach of normal ladders.

I would argue that in the suppression of unwelcome research reports, the rubbishing of academics' arguments, and the marginalising of unproductive pupils and schools we see a *further* erosion of democracy, and will see an increase of the underclass by virtue of the type of education system we are developing. (I am not, of course, suggesting that I wish incompetent schools to be left as they are – far from it; but a collegial system, which supports, *manages* and improves, would be far preferable to market forces, however they might operate here.)

Recent developments have also had a marked effect on the morale of the teaching profession. As Smithers and Robinson (1991) reported at the end of last year, 'Poor discipline, heavy workloads and lack of status are pushing teachers out of state schools and into the independent sector or out of education altogether' (*TES*, 27 December 1991, 'Lack of Status Fuels the Exodus'). Of those leaving the profession the highest proportion (a fifth) did so through early retirement or ill-health; typically ex-teachers became insurance-sellers, tour operators or taxi drivers, or opened guest houses (almost half of those leaving the profession became self-employed); more than half of those who decided to change jobs altogether said it was the feeling of being undervalued that prompted the decision. To those outside schools the teacher supply 'problem' seems to have gone away because recruitment to initial teacher training is buoyant. This is, however, seen within education to be due to the recession, rather than any sudden improvement in the status of teaching. As Professor Smithers put it the 'Government has solved the teacher supply crisis by closing down the economy.'

A.H. Halsey in his (third) survey of academic staff in Universities and Polytechnics has documented the *Decline of Donnish Dominion* (1992). During the last thirty years higher education has expanded on an enormous scale. One might have thought that with the growing demand for its services the status of the academic profession would have risen; instead, public esteem for academics is lower than ever. Our prestige has plummeted in the eyes of the 'politician and the populace': deteriorating conditions of intellectual work, declining autonomy of institutions, fallen salaries, decreased chances of promotion, loss of tenure – these are the tangible aspects of the loss of status and esteem. Few of Halsey's respondents now recommend to their students a life in higher education. Halsey ascribes this decline to the proletarianisation of intellectual labour; to 'dogmatic preferences for market solutions ... distorted by an urgent search for political survival and advantage'; and to increasing disagreement about what universities are for (Are they meant to transmit knowledge or enhance it; to provide useful knowledge or knowledge for its own sake; and is the primary aim to supply the economy with a technologically efficient work force?). Halsey's view is that one reason why the response from academics to this hostile climate has been so mild is because of their tolerance of hostile ideology and the patience to pursue reasoned argument. Perhaps it is time academics gave up these traits.

THE DIRECTION OF EDUCATIONAL REFORM

One result of the direction in which education and educational reform are moving is that we are putting ourselves firmly into a pedagogical and curriculum model (for the vast majority of pupils and schools, but, of course, not for the high status ones) which will not produce the sort of individual which this country needs for the next century.

The movement that we are seeing this century is social, political, cultural and economic, and education is charged with responding to this global change. However, it is the economic changes which drive the rhetoric: technological developments demand better educated, more thoughtful and flexible workers across the labour market, to strengthen the country's technological base and to foster a spirit of enterprise and initiative. The apparent mismatch between the output of the schools and the needs of the labour market, as indicated by the number of unqualified school leavers and by the number of young unemployed, suggested that education had departed from the 'real world' of work, and the result has been to seek to recouple education with the economy (Neave, 1988). This has resulted in a redefinition of the cultural base on which education rests, away from the humanistic tradition towards an industrial culture. Together with this comes a celebration of cultural uniformity, a return to a subject-bound, traditional curriculum and the transmission model of teaching within formal classrooms.

Traditional curricular and pedagogical models are at odds with what research in cognition is telling us: that learning is a process of knowledge construction, not of recording or absorption; that learning is knowledge-dependent – we use current knowledge to construct new knowledge; and that learning is highly tuned to the situation in which it takes place.

> Cognitive theories tell us that learning occurs not by recording information but by interpreting it. Effective learning depends on the intentions, self-monitoring, elaborations, and representational construc- tions of the individual learner. The traditional view of instruction as direct transfer of knowledge does not fit this constructivist perspective. We need instead instructional theories that place the learner's constructive mental activity at the heart of any instructional exchange, that treat instruction as an intervention in an ongoing knowledge construction process. This does not mean, however, that students can be left to discover everything for themselves. (Resnick, 1989)

In addition, it seems that the search for generalisable or transferable knowledge in producing the flexible learner could be better served by teaching strategies for successful learning. Successful learners tend to elaborate and develop self-explanations to extend the information they are dealing with; they also tend to monitor their own understanding as they work. These metacognitive strategies, together with the habit of meaning-imposition, tend to make individuals successful learners in a range of domains. The learner's intentional efforts to find links among elements of knowledge, to develop explanations and justifications, and to raise questions serve to produce the flexible learner better than a focus on transfer in basic processes or a search for packages of knowledge that have wide applicability.

Similarly, the more traditional model of classroom management in which the teacher manages the teaching (and learning) experience, and in which students are to be obedient, compliant learners, is in tension with our educational requirements for the next century – the self-motivated, active learner. Classroom management needs to do more than elicit predictable obedience: it should be a vehicle for the enhancement of self-understanding, self-evaluation and the internali-sation of self-control and direction (McCaslin and Good, 1992). This requires allowing pupils to have growing responsibility for and self-regulation in their learning and to become adaptive learners rather than predictable learners.

Current directions in central policy making in education are at odds with the directions which research on learning and cognition would tell us to take. The transmission model of teaching, in a traditional formal classroom, with strong subject and task boundaries and traditional narrow assessment, is the opposite of what we need to produce learners who can think critically, synthesize and transform, experiment and create. We need a flexible curriculum, active co-operative forms of learning, opportunities for pupils to talk through the knowledge which they are incorporating, open forms of assessment (e.g., self-evaluation and reflection on their learning); in short, a thinking curriculum aimed at higher order performance and cognitive skills.

Instead, we are heading, inexplicably, back to the grammar school curriculum (with the addition of computing and technology) in a system in which teachers, deprived of autonomy, will have little scope for offering learners autonomy in a high stakes testing-driven system. Teaching for understanding is, after all, not the same as teaching for the test.

References

DES (1991), *Testing Seven-Year-Olds in 1991: Results of the National Curriculum Assessments in England*, DES, London.

Dewey, J. (1915), *The School and Society*, University of Chicago Press, London.

Gipps, C. (1990), 'The Social Implications of National Assessment', *Urban Review*, vol. 22, no. 2.

Halsey, A.H. (1992), *The Decline of Donnish Dominion: the British Academic Professions in the Twentieth Century*, Oxford University Press, Oxford.

HMI (1988), *The Introduction of GCSE in Schools 1986-1988*, DES, London.

McCaslin, M. and Good, T. (1992), 'Compliant Cognition: The Misalliance of Management and Instructional Goals in Current School Reform', *Educational Researcher*, vol. 21, no. 3.

Neave, G. (1988), 'Education and Social Policy: Demise of an Ethic or Change of Values?', *Oxford Review of Education*, vol. 14, no. 3.
Resnick, L. (ed.), (1989), *Knowing, Learning and Instruction*, Lawrence Erlbaum Associates, New Jersey.
Smithers, A. and Robinson, P. (1991), *Teacher Turnover*, Manchester University Press, Manchester.

PART II

4

THE SHIFTING SCENERY OF THE NATIONAL CURRICULUM

PAUL J. BLACK, OBE KSG

Paul Black is Professor of Science Education at the Centre for Educational Studies at King's College, University of London. He was formerly Chair of the Task Group on Assessment and Testing (TGAT) and Deputy Chair of the National Curriculum Council and Chair of its Curriculum Review Committee. He is currently a member of the International Commission on Physics Education and consultant to the World Bank, to the National Science Foundation (USA) on its review of USA Science Education and to the OECD project on Science, Mathematics and Technology Education in its member countries.

We reproduce here Professor Black's presidential address to the Education Section of the British Association for the Advancement of Science meeting at the University of Southampton on 25 August 1992.

As in the case of Professor Bolton's address, although widely reported in the national and educational press, this address has not previously been reproduced in full.

A SWEEPING AND HURRIED CHANGE

The national curriculum and national assessment constitute a vast experiment. The entire schooling in our 25,000 schools for almost all children from ages five to sixteen is to be subject to radically new procedures. No other country in the world has a system which gives such comprehensive control to its government over the curriculum with such a frequent and closely controlled system of national assessment. Thus there are no precedents for our new system. There are ample reasons to be fearful about the way in which these sweeping powers may be exercised.

Yet the implementation of the system is being put through with great speed, so that within four years of the passing of the Education Reform Act, most of its important features are in place. There has therefore been no time for extensive trial of the new ideas. If this were a new drug, its application, even for those in dire need, would not be allowed with this degree of untried novelty.

This might all be justified if our education had been in a state of collapse before 1988. It clearly had some serious problems, but were they so bad that the only option for improvement was such an urgent and sweeping set of changes? Between 1970–71 and 1989–90 the percentage of pupils obtaining no graded examination results as school leavers fell from 44 per cent to 8.3 per cent (due in part to the raising of the school leaving age), while the percentage gaining five or more higher grades at GCSE or the older equivalents rose from 7.1 per cent to 11.4 per cent (DES, 1992). This hardly sounds like a story of dire failure.

The changes might be defended if they were to be accompanied by thorough and independent evaluation so that the programmes could be monitored and lessons learnt from the only experience that matters, that of pupils in classrooms. My own experience in the National Curriculum Council was that comprehensive programmes for monitoring were cut back by Ministers, who have retained for themselves direct control over any research or evaluation activities of that Council. All that was allowed were programmes with modest budgets aimed at exploring tightly defined questions. In consequence, evidence that the reforms as a whole might contain serious flaws cannot be forthcoming.

Nevertheless, at the same time, the orders in science and mathematics have been revised within two years of their original issue (DES, 1989; 1991). An exercise to propose similar changes for technology is now underway and the threat of a revision for English now hangs in the air. Moreover, the Secretary of State has drawn up the revisions, not on the basis of a year's work from a broadly based professional body, as for the original orders, but on the basis of a few month's work from a small and officially anonymous group drawn from the inspectorate. However well qualified its members may be, the practice of open government here, as elsewhere, is in retreat.

THE LOSS OF CONFIDENCE

These recent changes are very alarming portents. From my own close contacts among teachers in science education, I was confident, until the beginning of 1991, that the reforms were generally welcomed. Teachers were very worried about the burdens that the rapid implementation of change was placing on them. However, they accepted two things: the first was that the original definition of the national curriculum for science was educationally sound, and that the many new features that it introduced could give a big improvement in science education; the second was that greater uniformity in science education, together with sensitive methods of assessment, could lead to all pupils being better guided throughout their learning of the subject.

This consensus has now changed. Teachers who had spent, in 1989, many hours of extra work in a total reorganisation of their teaching schemes for science and who, in 1991, were just in the second year of putting these into practice, discovered that there was to be a change. The changes turned out to be very extensive, so that all of their work of planning had to be done again. At the annual conference of the Association for Science Education in January 1992, the atmosphere of anger and cynicism was evident. A system that could make changes so quickly, without regard to its effects on their work, clearly did not appreciate or care about their professional efforts. They were drawing an even more corrosive lesson: it isn't worth taking the national curriculum too seriously any more because it'll probably be changed again in a year or two.

The rapid changes do not seem to be grounded in evidence. The limited evaluations possible during the first year of implementation for the science and mathematics and English orders, both by the HMI and by the National Curriculum Council, both referred to the improvements in school work and neither made out any case that the orders needed changing quickly.

THE DEMISE OF THE TGAT REPORT

However, the aspect of change on which I wish to concentrate is national assessment. As chair of the Task Group on Assessment and Testing which reported to Kenneth Baker in January 1988 (DES, 1988), I have watched the reception and subsequent implementation of that group's recommendations with particular concern.

Our report to the Minister was published very speedily. Margaret Thatcher's views were published very quickly afterwards, her concerns being revealed by way of a leak to the opposition spokesperson on education. During the next few months, both I and most other members of the task group gave a large number of talks, to the annual conferences of all of the main professional organisations in education, to various HMI meetings and to many local courses and conferences. We were greeted, in the press and at these meetings, with widespread approval for the recommendations. At no time was I faced with serious arguments for rejecting the main proposals, either in public print or at public meetings.

After a few months of public debate and Government silence, Kenneth Baker made an announcement in the House of Commons broadly accepting the TGAT recommendations. The 1989 DES booklet, *From Policy to Practice* (DES, 1989), reported his commitment and set out a three-page account of the main elements of the national assessment system.

Satisfaction at this outcome has been slowly but surely eroded. It is clear that most of the undertakings given in 1989 have by now, three years and three Secretaries of State later, been abandoned. I propose to deal with three questions that arise from this outcome. What has happened? Does it matter? How did it happen?

WHAT HAS HAPPENED?

This is a story of death by a thousand cuts. It would be tedious to describe all the changes in detail. I shall summarise the main points in numbered order as follows – the quotations in italics are from the 1989 DES document:

1. *'Teachers' own assessments are an essential part of the system.'*

The proportion of SEAC's resources devoted to researching and developing teachers' formative assessment has been tiny. The DES document in 1989 referred to the good practice on teacher assessment 'developed in recent years in the GCSE'. But we know by now that this good practice is no longer trusted in the way that it used to be.

2. *'Pupils achievements will not be displayed against each attainment target but the report will show the level they are at in terms of the overall profile component.'*

SEAC subsequently declared that pupils' results would have to be reported against every separate attainment target. The Secretary of State had by then put through orders with seventeen targets in science and fourteen in mathematics. It seemed absurd to me that SEAC could contemplate reporting separately on such a large number, but it was not until the examining groups pointed out that they could not possibly do this at GCSE level with any respectable degree of accuracy that the absurdity was accepted. So the orders for science and mathematics had to be revised to cut these numbers down.

Yet this problem should have been foreseen. In 1987-88, the Education Reform Bill was being put through Parliament by a ministerial team and their advisers who were at the same time monitoring the progress of the groups working to specify these large numbers of targets for science and mathematics. The need for a small number was never mentioned, and the Minister put the large number versions through after the Act had been finally passed. It is not possible to say who was responsible for this expensive confusion, but it is clear that thousands of science teachers, and especially the most dedicated, have – through the disruption from the later changes – suffered as a result.

3. *'Assessment should be by a combination of national external tests and assessment by teachers'* [and, talking later about the teacher's record of pupils' progress] *'. . . it may be important evidence to bring to bear in moderation discussions.'*

Readers of this would assume that this was an intention to implement the TGAT recommendations, which was that the results of the two forms of assessment should be combined for every reported target. They have been cruelly misled: external tests are to be the only evidence except in the case of practical and performance attainment targets, for which teachers' assessment will be the only evidence.

4. *'Standard assessment tasks will be designed to be a support for learning, and will be drawn up under the direction of SEAC with the classroom context very much in mind. SATs for key stage 1 will each test attainment in a range of foundation subjects and will be designed to be administered unobtrusively. Teachers will be able to select from a bank of SATs those which most closely fit the sort of work they have been doing with their pupils.'*

Such an approach was developed to the stage of extensive trials in primary schools. Some teachers complained about the workload, and, as complainants do, received more attention from the media than those who found them both challenging and helpful to their teaching practices. There was no public complaint when the key stage 3 trials were carried out to test the same principles. However, Kenneth Clarke quickly declared the new tests to be unacceptable and laid down new principles.

Of the new key stage 1 tests, an editorial in *Child Education* for August 1992 said: 'Although the tests were simplified, teachers still found them time-consuming and disruptive, while in the name of manageability they had sacrificed the more interesting and worthwhile activities.' Those developing the key stage 3 science SAT's for 1991 had asked all teachers involved to fill in feedback questionnaires about the proposed assessments and to give their opinions about various changes that could be made. The new principles embody changes to which teachers were opposed, and have abandoned many elements which commanded widespread support from teachers.

In setting out this summary, I have not used the TGAT report, but the Government's own publicity commitments, as the point of reference. I do this because the point to be underlined is not that TGAT lost the argument. We won the argument. The chilling feature is, that in the world of political pressure to which education is now subject, that was of no consequence.

DOES IT MATTER?

It could still be argued that all of these retreats are indeed improvements won by hard evidence of the impracticability of the original proposals. I would argue to the contrary that the current ideas are based on prejudice rather than evidence and are set fair to do serious harm to children's education.

Don't change too quickly.

On the basis of evidence about the original plans there is no argument. None of the retreats has been based on comprehensive evidence of practices in schools, let alone on analysis of the performances of pupils or of the opinions of teachers. Moreover, anyone who has been involved closely in curriculum innovation, as I have been, learns that the first year of implementation can provide evidence for minor adjustments but cannot give valid evidence to justify large changes, except where there is a serious breakdown. The reason is simple: it is only when teachers have had the time to incorporate changes into their own classroom practice that the potential, for good or ill, of an innovation can be appraised.

There is a substantial literature on innovation and change in education, notably summarised in the writing of Michael Fullan, of the University of Toronto (Fullan, 1991). One clear lesson from many studies is this: changes imposed from outside which teachers are not able to take to heart and make their own are ineffective. This is not to plead that governments should be nice to teachers and respect them – although that would be a good idea – put to point out that mere imposition from outside just does not work. A teacher is in sensitive personal contact with many individual children, and has to develop his or her role by fashioning a personal style to deal with the multiple and exhausting pressures that bear on the classroom, both inside it and from outside it. You cannot treat such a person as a robot to be reprogrammed.

'PROPER TESTS'

I start with a quotation from Kenneth Clarke from the Westminster Lecture which he gave in June 1991 (Clarke, 1991) when he was Secretary of State.

> The British pedagogue's hostility to written examinations of any kind can be taken to ludicrous extremes. The British left believe that 'pencil and paper' examinations impose stress on pupils and demotivate them. We have tolerated for twenty years an arrangement whereby there is no national testing or examination of any kind for most pupils until they face GCSE at the age of sixteen . . . This remarkable national obsession lies behind the more vehement opposition to the recent introduction of seven-year-old testing. They were made a little too complicated and we have said we will simplify them . . . The complications themselves were largely designed in the first place in an attempt to pacify opponents who feared above all else 'paper and pencil' tests . . . This opposition to testing and examinations is largely based on a folk memory in the left about the old debate on the eleven-plus and grammar schools.

I want to spend a little time on this paragraph, because it shows several of the characteristics of the current political rhetoric. The 'complicated' seven-year-old testing to which this extract refers was recommended by TGAT. The 'complication' was a proposal that the tests be designed as pieces of classroom activity rather like a good teaching activity. Children would take some time to become involved in the activity, but then it would be so designed that they would be required to produce some writing, some number work, some measurements and so on. Thus, in the context of the work, each child would produce evidence of his or her capacity to meet the various attainment targets of the foundation subject. The TGAT's reasons for proposing this arose from a desire to make the seven-year-old testing valid and effective. The formal timed test is a strange occasion, and any child's performance will depend strongly on skills in writing for an ill-defined audience and on his or her capacity to understand what this strange situation is about.

Our concern was two-fold. First that such tests would not give a reliable picture of what a child could do. It is evident with adults that their performance in work may be either much stronger or much weaker than their performance in a short test or interview designed to select them for that work. Staff appraisal schemes review work performance; it would be ludicrous to suggest that these use written tests instead. If this is so for adults, how much more true must it be for seven-year-old children whose capacities to communicate and to understand the significance of what is happening to them are so much more limited? Of course, the capacity to write must be assessed, but if a child is strong in other areas but weak in written expression, it is misleading if the strengths are not revealed because of reliance on only one mode of communication.

Second, any external tests are bound to exert pressure on teaching methods: teachers will be tempted to drill pupils to perform in the tests. The aim, therefore, must be to make the test such that preparation and rehearsal is a good way of learning. So the assessments were designed to be models of good learning with assessment firmly built in. Since we also believed that classroom assessment by teachers was an area of weakness, it was hoped that these well designed pieces would be models of good practice. I believe that they were and that those who complained about the workload were actually struggling to get hold of a more stringent model of teaching and assessment than they had been used to.

All of this reasoning was in the TGAT report. It is deeply disturbing to have it rejected because it was 'complicated' and because it was 'designed to pacify opponents'. I do not mind if our arguments are confronted with counter-argument and evidence, but I find it offensive to have them attacked by imputation of the motives of the group which

I chaired. The imputation is in any event strange. The group included, with myself and others, people who had for many years been responsible for paper and pencil tests taken by hundreds of thousands of pupils in our public examination systems, in APU testing, and in the numerous standardised and diagnostic tests used by schools. We knew far more about paper and pencil testing than any of the right-wing critics; in particular, we were well aware of their strengths and of their weaknesses and were struggling to use that expertise to fashion an optimum system.

The second feature of the arguments in the passage is even more disturbing. Opposition and opposing arguments are lumped together. If one asks, 'Who is being attacked here?', then it appears that in the first line it is 'The British pedagogue'; on the next line this becomes 'The British left'. Near the end, there is a clear reference to the TGAT group. The reasons given by some groups, which were not TGAT's reasons, are lumped together in a single linked wave of criticism. This stereotyping of all expert opinion and evidence is very common in political argument. The effect that I have noticed is that many of us who really believe in the value of tough and reliable assessments are being bracketed together with those opposed to all testing, and are thereby labelled as woolly-minded. I fear that critics in government do not really understand the deep difference between those who want to break away from traditional tests in order to improve assessment and testing because they care about it, and those who want to abandon it altogether.

The result of such indiscriminate arguments will be a return to tests of poor validity, dangerous unreliability and with a heritage of damaging effects on pupils' learning. It is not clear why these traditional tests are so preferred. It appears that they bear the image of 'traditional values' in this field, that they might have the advantage that teachers who are not to be trusted are not involved in them, perhaps even that they must be good because the 'pedagogues' and/or the 'left' don't like them.

ASSESSMENT AND LEARNING

I have spent over two of the last four months in the USA. The practice of assessment there is undergoing a rapid change. The use of short external standardised tests, almost always multiple choice tests, has been widespread for several decades, and the technical expertise in developing these has reached a far higher level than anywhere else in the world. However, many of the States are now abandoning them, because it is evident that they have done almost nothing to improve education. Since 1989, sixteen of the States have started to develop and implement alternative forms of assessment in science, twenty in mathematics; and a review, in spring this year, said that further new initiatives are developing rapidly (Blank and Dalkilic, 1992).

Their new interest is in tests of performance, which are closer to good classroom practice, which take longer to use, and in which teachers can be fully involved. One of their chief sources of ideas in this drive to find more valid and useful forms of assessment has been Great Britain. The work of many agencies here, and particularly the reports of the Assessment of Performance Unit (APU) are well known and much used. The TGAT report is also well known. I have spoken to many of those involved in these changes. They are astonished to hear what is now happening here: they see us as marching backwards into the unprofitable ways from which they are now escaping. Ironically, one of their chief objects of admiration – the APU – was an initiative of our Government. Its lessons had a profound effect on the TGAT deliberations. They are now influencing the US policies, though they appear to have little, if any, effect on our own Government's policy.

I would like to expand on this point a little more. First, let me give an assurance – my reporting of trends in the USA does not derive from chats with a few academic friends. I have been invited to take part in consultations with the State Departments of Education in California and in Connecticut; I have been involved, with foreign experts from other countries, in formulating policy advice for the National Science Foundation; and I have worked as the only overseas invited expert on a committee of the US National Academy of Sciences, charged with drawing up advice on assessment standards for a new national statement on the future science curriculum for US schools.

I can illustrate the nature of the current concerns in the USA by quoting from the most recent authoritative book on the subject, entitled *Changing Assessments: Alternative Views of Aptitude Achievement and Instruction* (Gifford and O'Connor, 1992). This is a collection of studies by twelve leading authorities in the USA, produced under the aegis of their National Commission on Testing and Public Policy and published earlier this year. Here, first of all, are three quotations from a closing summary by Professor Lorrie Shepard:

The most important contribution ... is the insight that all learning involves thinking. It is incorrect to believe, according to old learning theory, that the basics can be taught by rote followed by thinking and reasoning. As documented by the Resnicks, even comprehension of simple texts requires a process of inferring and thinking about what the text means. Children who are drilled in number facts, algorithms, decoding skills or vocabulary lists without developing a basic conceptual model or seeing the meaning of what they are doing have a very difficult time retaining information (because all the bits are disconnected) and are unable to apply what they have memorised (because it makes no sense).

'Measurement-driven instruction' will lead reform in the wrong direction if tests embody incomplete or low-level learning goals.

Various efforts to reform assessment use terms such as 'authentic', 'direct' and 'performance' assessment to convey the idea that assessments must capture real learning activities if they are to avoid distorting instruction. (Shepard, 1992)

The article by Resnick and Resnick, to which Shepard refers, develops a critique of the multiple choice or very short answer tests which were until recently almost the only form of testing in US schools:

Children who practise reading mainly in the form in which it appears in the tests – and there is good evidence that this is what happens in many classrooms – would have little exposure to the demands and reasoning possibilities of the thinking curriculum.

Students who practised mathematics in the form found in the standardized tests would never be exposed to the kind of mathematical thinking sought by all who are concerned with reforming mathematical education . . . (Resnick and Resnick, 1992)

The article goes on to emphasise the inevitable effects on teaching of any tests designed for accountability purposes, and concludes:

Assessments must be so designed that when you do the natural thing – that is, prepare the students to perform well – they will exercise the kinds of abilities and develop the kinds of skills that are the real goals of educational reform. (Resnick and Resnick, 1992)

The article then describes assessments which would have a positive effect on teaching. Of the three examples given, one is the teacher assessed project in the former JMB Engineering Science and a second was a test of higher order thinking skills devised by NAEP (the US National Assessment of Educational Progress) which drew heavily on APU science items and for which one of my APU science team was a consultant. The authors conclude that:

If widely adopted as part of the public accountability assessment system, performance assessments (including portfolio assessments) could not only remove current pressures for teaching isolated collections of facts and skills but also provide a positive stimulus for introducing more extended thinking and reasoning activities in the curriculum. (Resnick and Resnick, 1992)

Finally, another quotation from Shepard which could have been written as a commentary on the current position in this country:

If they are unaware of new research findings about how children learn, policy-makers are apt to rely on their own implicit theories which were most probably shaped by the theories that were current when they themselves attended school . . . Some things that psychologists can prove today even contradict the popular wisdom of several decades ago. Therefore, if policy-makers proceed to implement outmoded theories or tests based on old theories, they might actually subvert their intended goal – of providing a rigorous and high quality education for all students. (Shepard, 1992)

ASSESSMENT IN THE CLASSROOM

I do not agree with all of the arguments of the Resnicks in the work quoted above. They want to emphasise the difference between external accountability tests and teachers' own assessments. However, their arguments are in all other respects very close to the TGAT arguments. They emphasise the need to develop teachers' formative assessment and the need for summative assessments to be as faithful to good learning practice as possible.

The point I want to emphasise here is that, because teachers know their pupils well and can assess their progress on many and varied occasions over a long time, they are in a far better position to make a more authentic and reliable assessment of a pupil's work than any external test can achieve. If such assessments are valued and play a significant part in accountability assessments, then the undesirable effects of testing on good learning can be avoided. However, a great deal needs to be invested in developing good practice in formative assessment.

It was also clear to the TGAT group that external assessments must also be used to calibrate teachers' own assessments, while discrepancies between the two ought to be discussed with groups of teachers by a set procedure for resolving differences in the light of evidence. Such monitoring meetings are known to be of great professional value to all involved. All of this has been rejected, and it does seem as if those rejecting it do not understand the limitations of external tests and do not share the TGAT view of the prime importance of improving the practice and the status of teachers' formative assessments as essential to good teaching and learning. Another quote from Shepard reinforces the point here:

> ... the teacher has need of constant information about what the student knows and the strategies being used to process and comprehend new concepts ... By imbedding diagnostic instruction in instructional activities, teachers can preserve the integrity of assessment tasks (the wholeness of tasks and natural learning context) and protect instructional time that would otherwise be diverted to testing ... There is general agreement that external packaged tests will not solve the problem of what teachers need to know about student learning. (Shepard, 1992)

The APU assessments were related as closely as possible to the best classroom practice, but went ahead of it in showing how new aims could be assessed faithfully. The new assessment methods and items so developed have been welcomed and used by many teachers. Many of these new methods cannot be implemented in the short, time-limited external test.

The TGAT group were well aware that short, time-limited external tests are bound to emphasise isolated and disconnected pieces of knowledge. We also were concerned that such emphasis was bound to feed back into the classroom and put teachers under pressure to teach for such tests, a practice which would do damage to good learning practice. Drawing on arguments very similar to those quoted above, and on the extensive development of good assessment experiences in this country, the TGAT report tried to open up the possibility that a new positive relation between good teaching and good assessment could be developed. That prospect is now receding, and drilling for the test is now taking its place – to the dismay of many teachers and the potential impoverishment of many pupils.

CAN THE RESULTS BE TRUSTED?

The reliability of tests which are used to judge schools and to influence the future of pupils must clearly be a matter of great concern. To take an example, at key stage 3 pupils' national assessment in three of the four attainment targets in science will be settled by a single three-hour test, externally set and written as a formal timed examination. The test has to produce results separately on each of the three targets, which gives one hour per target. The question at issue is, can such a short test produce an answer that can be trusted?

In the APU work, considerable effort was devoted to finding out how reliable the survey results were. It was shown that if a pupil was set two different sets of questions designed to test the same thing, the results could be very different. To choose either one of them to label that pupil would be unfair because of the inaccuracy. The average of the two, or better still, the results of a test using more questions, could give a better estimate. The technical results of such studies have been published by the DES itself (DES, 1988). There is nothing new about such results: everyone knows that examination results can be inaccurate, and when pupils could take the same subject with two different GCE boards, reports of wide differences in some of the results were commonplace.

It is also clear that the shorter the test, the less reliable its result can be. From all the evidence that I know from my involvement in the APU science work, the result of one hour of testing on science performance in an attainment target will be untrustworthy. To cover the ground, the test will be bound to adopt those narrow forms of test items which the US State authorities are abandoning after decades of experience with them.

Data on the reliability of the 1990 and 1991 pilots and trials of the SATs have not been published, and the new versions, being shorter in time, will probably be less reliable. At a public presentation, given in January 1992 by SEAC officers, about these new science tests, I asked what studies would be undertaken to determine how reliable the new tests will be. I was told that there would be none. I asked whether that meant that there would be no data available to the public about how reliable the test results will be. I was told that in my sense of the word reliability, that was so. The sense in which I was asking about reliability was about whether a pupil taking an identical test, or a similar test, such as, for example, might be set for the SAT next year, would be likely or not to get the same result on both tests. Clearly, if the chances for this are low, the test result will be worthless and teachers, pupils and parents will be well advised to ignore the results.

HOW DID IT HAPPEN?

I am not able to give more than a few indications towards an answer to this question. We could all do so if the changes that have occurred to the policy announced in *From Policy to Practice* had happened as an outcome of reasoned public debate, but that has not been the case. We could do so if evidence to support the new strategies had been quoted and could be examined. There has been little evidence, but many broad assertions.

Eric Bolton, in his recent speech (reprinted in this volume), has drawn attention to the overwhelming influence, on current government policy in education, of the right-wing pressure groups, notably the Centre for Policy Studies. One of its leading figures replaced the dismissed chairman of SEAC. It is now clear that the changes to the memberships of the national councils for the curriculum and for assessment give each of these an increasing bias towards that particular element in our governing party. Because of this, the teaching profession is rapidly losing any serious respect for these councils.

The hopes of many that the Government would exercise its sole power to appoint to the councils in an impartial way have been sharply disappointed. Those who gave dire warnings that the Education Reform Act would be an instrument for direct government control, in which the opinions of ministers would be insulated from professional opinion and expertise, have been proved correct.

Of course, it may be that the bulk of that opinion and expertise is deeply in error. In the pressure groups' rhetoric, the so-called educational establishment has been elevated to the status of bogeyman, and the terms 'expert', 'academic' and 'researcher' have been turned into terms of abuse. As an expert academic researcher who saw the Act as a force for good, and who has given much of his time to trying to help its development, I am deeply disappointed and fearful at the outcomes I have described in this paper.

However, if it is true that the judgements and experience of the entire 'educational establishment' have to be dismissed, then we really are in very profound trouble. If the teaching profession's practices and judgements are no longer to be trusted, then the fault cannot be corrected simply by giving them new orders. They are not robots. All who care for education should not want them to be robots. To treat them as if they were robots is to run the risk that they will start to behave as robots should.

REFERENCES

Blank, R.K. and Dalkilic, M. (1992), *State Policies on Science and Mathematics Education*, Council of Chief State School Officers, Washington, DC, USA.

Child Education (1992), *Editorial Comment*, vol. 69, no. 8, p4, Scholastic Publications, Leamington Spa.

Clarke, K (1991), *Education in a Classless Society*, The Westminster Lecture given to the Tory Reform Group, June 1991.

DES (1988), *Task Group on Assessment and Testing: A Report*, DES, London.

DES (1989), *National Curriculum: From Policy to Practice*, DES, London.

DES (1989), *Science in the National Curriculum 1989*, HMSO, London.

DES (1991), *Science in the National Curriculum 1991*, HMSO, London.

DES (1992), *Statistical Bulletin 3/92*, DES, London.

Fullan, M.G. with Stiegelbauer, S. (1991), *The New Meaning of Educational Change*, Cassell, London.

Gifford, B.R. and O'Connor, M.C. (1992), *Changing Assessments: Alternative Views of Aptitude, Achievement and Instruction*, Kluwer, Boston and Dordrecht.

Johnson, S. (1988), *National Assessment: the APU Science Approach*, HMSO, London.

Resnick, L.R. and Resnick, D.P. (1992), 'Assessing the Thinking Curriculum: New Tools for Educational Reform', pp37–75 in Gifford and O'Connor (*op.cit.*).

Shepard, L.A. (1992), 'Commentary: What Policy Makers Who Mandate Tests Should Know About the New Psychology of Intellectual Ability and Learning', pp301–28 in Gifford and O'Connor (*op.cit.*).

5

IS THERE COHERENCE AND PURPOSE IN THE NATIONAL CURRICULUM?

DENIS LAWTON

Denis Lawton was formerly Director of the University of London Institute of Education where he is currently Professor of Education specialising in education planning and curriculum studies. His recent books include Curriculum Studies and Educational Planning *(1983),* Education, Culture and the National Curriculum *(1989) and* Education and Politics in the 1990s: Conflict or Consensus? *(1992) The address reproduced here was given to the Education Section of the British Association for the Advancement of Science meeting at the University of Southampton on 25 August 1992.*

The question in the title that I was asked to address can be answered very briefly: coherence – no; purpose – yes, but the purpose was mainly political.

I will spend most of the rest of the time justifying that answer, in terms of two more concepts 'ideology' and 'implementation'.

BACKGROUND

A national curriculum was not on the political agenda until the mid-1980s. The ideologically different notion of a common curriculum had been on the *educational* agenda for much longer (Council for Curriculum Reform, 1945; Williams, 1961; Lawton, 1973); and HMI had been discussing the desirability of an entitlement curriculum from the early 1970s, and especially since *Curriculum 11-16* (1977). But that approach to curriculum planning should also be seen as quite distinct from the national curriculum 1988: the HMI strategy would have been persuasion and gentle dissemination rather than the kind of legislation for a top-down curriculum which appeared in 1988.

It may be helpful to look in a little more detail at the years 1979-92.

First of all, it is not without significance that during those thirteen years of Conservative rule, there have been two Prime Ministers, and, more importantly, six Secretaries of State for Education:

1979-81: Mark Carlisle apparently showed little interest in the idea of a national curriculum, and spent his time struggling to retain a reasonable share of the reducing public expenditure (and carving out enough money for the Assisted Places Scheme).

1981-86: Keith Joseph was ideologically opposed to the idea of a national curriculum which was, however, raised for discussion in his time (*Better Schools*, in 1985, explicitly rejected a national curriculum).

1986-89: Kenneth Baker was the enthusiast for and driving force behind the national curriculum. He seized upon the idea eagerly and wanted results very quickly – for reasons we can only speculate about. But the haste was destructive. And, ironically, despite the haste, Baker did not have the chance of putting his plan into operation: he was 'promoted' in 1989 to the Chairmanship of the Party.

1989-90: John MacGregor was left with the job of implementation. He was beginning to appreciate the difficulties and the complexities involved (some say he listened; others say he 'went native'). He was moved on.

1990-92: Kenneth Clarke was appointed by Margaret Thatcher to apply the same kind of diplomatic skills to education that had been so successful in the NHS. He wanted commonsense simplicity, an end to 'elaborate nonsense'.

April 1992- : John Patten? We must wait and see.

THE EDUCATION REFORM ACT (1988) AND AFTER

In discussing the national curriculum, we are really talking about a very brief period: from Kenneth Baker's 'North of England Speech' in January 1987 to 1992 – less than six years: a short time in education, but a very long time in politics. I keep stressing the time factor because it is such an important part of the analysis of implementation.

I must now return to the two questions in the title: coherence and purpose. I will start with purpose: why did Kenneth Baker want a national curriculum? What were the social, political and educational intentions behind the initiative? The main purpose of this paper is to try to explain *why* politicians went in a direction which was to prove to be so disastrously wrong.

On 9 January 1987 Kenneth Baker, as Secretary of State, made a speech to the North of England Conference in Rotherham (DES, 1987). He suggested that the English education system was 'eccentric' – less centralised than that of France and Germany. He complained that standards were not high enough and that there was lack of agreement over a curriculum for the fourteen to sixteen age group:

> These weaknesses do not arise in those West European countries where the schools follow more or less standard syllabuses. In those countries the school system produces results which overall are at least as satisfactory as those produced here; and the teachers are no less professional than ours. Nor do these countries show any sign of wanting to give up the advantages of national syllabuses.

That statement was not completely correct: Baker ignored the fact that many countries with centralised curricula were trying to free schools from *too much* central control. But, if you take out the attempt at persuasive rhetoric, Kenneth Baker was simply saying that he wanted a school system that was more efficient, with higher standards and with better accountability.

This does not seem to be an unreasonable set of intentions . . . what went wrong? In making some criticisms I would like to stress that I am *not* opposed to the principle of a national curriculum – I have been arguing in favour of some kind of national guidelines for the last twenty years.

PROBLEMS OF DEVISING AND IMPLEMENTING THE NATIONAL CURRICULUM

There are at least three explanations for the problems that arose: *ideological* contradictions within the Conservative Party; *operational* problems about the national curriculum – it was bureaucratic not professional; *implementation* strategies were ignored or not understood. It may be helpful to look at each of them a little more closely.

Ideological Contradictions: Secretaries of State for Education, like other Cabinet Ministers, but perhaps more so, have to gain support from all sides of the Party. I have elsewhere (1989) suggested that there are four (overlapping) ideological positions on education which would have been important for curriculum planning, at least three of which could be found in the Conservative Party in 1987. Counting from the right:

1. *Privatisers*, who would prefer to abolish state schools and let people pay for what they want and can afford; they want market forces to operate in education.

2. *Minimalists*, who accept the need for state schooling but choose not to use it for their own children, and prefer the state to provide something less expensive; they tend to talk about 'the basics' and see schooling in terms of training for work rather than general education.

3. *Pluralists*, who would like state education to be so good that there would be no motive for having private schools; nevertheless, they argue in favour of the continued existence of independent schools on grounds of social diversity, freedom of choice and academic differentiation.

4. *Comprehensive Planners*, who would like to plan for a single system catering for all social and intellectual types of children. If there were any 'comprehensive planners' in the Conservative Party in 1987-88, they kept their heads down.

A curriculum is often a compromise, but some compromises involve contradictions and confusion rather than coherence. The kind of national curriculum envisaged or regarded as acceptable within the Conservative Party varied according to ideological position; and Kenneth Baker also had to convince his Cabinet colleagues that he had not been corrupted by his department. Thus the national curriculum *content* was expressed in a very conventional way indeed – a list of subjects that any MP would immediately recognise and regard as 'sound commonsense'. The HMI Entitlement Curriculum Model (based on 'Areas of Experience' rather than subjects) was ignored. It was unfamiliar and looked suspiciously like 'educational theory' – an increasingly taboo concept.

But the 'list of subjects' approach to curriculum was considered by most curriculum experts to be quite inappropriate for the 1990s: so many vital issues (for example, health education and political awareness) were not included in the subject structure; hence the repair work now being embarked upon by the National Curriculum Council in the field of cross-curricular themes.

Curriculum experts were carefully ignored in 1987; but assessment experts could not be. The different sections of the Conservative Party were promised greater national accountability *and* more market competition. A new assessment system was needed which could deliver data demonstrating the efficiency (or lack of it) in every state school, as well as providing test scores which could be used *competitively* and published in league table form (thus satisfying minimalists as well as privatisers). I will return to this under 'implementation'.

So much for the ideological contradictions; now for the second set of difficulties: *Operational Problems*. The national curriculum was bureaucratic rather than professional. (This is not unconnected with the points made about ideology above.) There is a mass of literature showing that successful curriculum change should start from the professional concerns of teachers, making use of their knowledge and experience, rather then as a top-down plan imposed on teachers by civil servants. Since 1988 teachers have increasingly felt deskilled and demoralised as a result of national curriculum arrangements. No attempt was made to give them 'joint ownership' of either the curriculum or its assessment. Most teachers behaved very professionally and did their best with the unsatisfactory curriculum model; but, although the principle of a National Curriculum is now generally accepted, they still regard the 1988 version as something alien which has to be accommodated.

The idea of a national curriculum was a tremendous opportunity: but it was a missed opportunity, largely because teachers *were* treated as hirelings to be given instructions rather than as professionals to be involved at all stages and at all levels. This could easily have been foreseen and avoided. Another bureaucratic mistake was to move from very general aims to lists of content expressed as objectives (or 'statements of attainment') without any intervening justification or explanation. This represented a serious error of curriculum design which should have been avoided.

My third explanation for the problems is concerned with *Implementation Strategies*. A good deal is now known about problems of ideal and reality – about the dangers of the gaps between planning and the realisation of those plans.

In many parts of the world (OECD Report, 1988) hard lessons have been learned about the difficulty of transferring splendid curriculum ideas into practice. The reasons for the difficulties of implementing curriculum change are no longer a mystery: the practical problems are extremely well documented (e.g., Fullan, 1982). And it would have been possible to overcome them.

The national curriculum itself, although very traditional, did involve some difficult changes: for example, fitting more subjects into the fourteen to sixteen timetable, and making sure that enough teachers would be available for subjects such as technology and modern languages. Such problems were ignored, and only when the results of the technology curriculum began to be particularly disastrous was action taken to rethink the nature of the subject and how it might be taught by existing teachers.

Even more importantly, from an implementation point of view, the excellent assessment scheme devised by the Task Group for Assessment and Testing should have involved:

(a) adequate time for co-ordination between the subject working groups (because time was so short, they simply went their own way, without comparing notes – and clarifying concepts – with other groups);

(b) time for making teachers familiar with the new ideas and procedures;

(c) time and resources for adequate training and moderation exercises (for both Teacher Assessment and Standard Assessment Tasks).

The most common error in the implementation of curriculum change is to underestimate the time and resources needed. The 1988 national curriculum will undoubtedly go down in history as a classic case of neglecting the lessons of previous studies.

For the national curriculum itself, several changes have been made, watering down the idea of entitlement to a new list of subjects with varying priorities. From fourteen to sixteen students may now choose to drop either History or Geography, and Music and Art have become completely optional. The idea of Entitlement for five to sixteen-year-olds has been removed: the Pluralists lost out to Minimalists and Privatisers.

Moreover, the national curriculum subject working groups developed incompatible concepts of 'Profile Components' and 'Attainment Targets' (ATs) which resulted in the mathematics and science ATs having to be reconsidered in 1991; the number of ATs was reduced from fourteen and seventeen to five and four – just when teachers were beginning to get familiar with the Mark I model.

As for assessment, because of inadequate time and resources, the crucial concept of Standard Assessment Tasks (SATs) has been distorted and replaced by short tests. Let me elaborate on that particular issue: the TGAT model of assessment possessed a number of advantages, even conceptual innovations of considerable power. Central to the new concept of assessment was the Standard Assessment Task. The SAT was intended to be a form of assessment which would avoid many of the disadvantages of conventional 'paper and pencil' tests (not least for seven-year-olds). The idea was that good examples of teaching-learning situations would be used by teachers in a standard way with built-in assessment opportunities for the teachers. Such assessment would not need to be either disruptive or intrusive. Some politicians (and maybe civil servants) were always suspicious about this approach which was eventually dismissed as 'elaborate nonsense' by Kenneth Clarke and replaced by more conventional tests – with all the disadvantages that TGAT had tried to avoid, and with little hope of validity and reliability (as Paul Black pointed out in his presidential address, reprinted in this volume).

THE ALTERNATIVE

So far this talk has been rather negative, criticising the politicians and some civil servants for their ignorance and impatience. What might have happened with better planning and forethought?

It would have been sensible to have encouraged and extended the

HMI experiments with LEAs on school-based curriculum development using the 'entitlement curriculum' as a set of guidelines for improving practice.

The assessment programme could have been introduced over a much longer period, allowing for the work of the individual subject groups to be co-ordinated, rather than each going their own way.

The national curriculum for five- to sixteen-year-olds could have been planned to integrate not only with the GCSE but also with the developments for the sixteen to nineteen age group.

It would have been possible to have worked *with* teachers rather than *against* them, giving them partial ownership of the curriculum and assessment procedures.

THE WAY FORWARD NOW?

It is important that teachers now are given every possible opportunity to make the existing curriculum structure work, even if it is a less than perfect model. Changes should be made only to remove intolerable bureaucratic burdens or to put right innovations which are professionally unacceptable. The major example of this kind is that test results should no longer be used to compare LEAs, schools and teachers themselves. Comparisons based on raw scores, regardless of the standards of the pupils in the first place, are clearly misleading and unfair. In the long run there would be advantages in separating the two functions of assessment by returning to APU testing (on the basis of light sampling *not* testing every child) to monitor standards, and use national curriculum assessment for formative and diagnostic purposes.

CONCLUSION

The lesson which emerges from the 1988 national curriculum is that educational planning – and, in particular, curriculum planning – is a very complex process and should not be attempted with political timetables. There will always be occasions when politicians spot a problem and are tempted to seek a 'quick fix'. They should be strongly advised against such temptations. In education there are very few problems which lend themselves to the 'quick fix' kind of solution. Politicians have a legitimate interest in the curriculum, but when it comes to making the system work they should be guided by those who know something about it, rather than by ill-informed, extremist views of political advisers.

REFERENCES

Council for Curriculum Reform (1945), *The Content of Education* University of London Press, London.
DES (1977), *Curriculum 11-16*, HMSO, London.
DES (1985), *Better Schools*, HMSO, London.
DES (1987), Secretary of State's Speech to North of England Conference, DES Press Release, London.
DES (1988), *National Curriculum Task Group for Assessment and Testing, First Report*, DES, London.
Fullan, M. (1982), *The Meaning of Educational Change*, Cassell, London.
Lawton, D. (1973), *Social Change, Educational Theory and Curriculum Planning*, Hodder & Stoughton, London.
Lawton, D. (1989), *Education, Culture and the National Curriculum*, Hodder & Stoughton, London.
Lawton, D. (1992), *Education and Politics in the 1990s: Conflict or Consensus?*, Falmer Press, Brighton.
OECD (1988), *School Development and New Approaches for Learning: Trends and Issues in Curriculum Reform*, OECD, Paris.
Williams, R. (1961), *The Long Revolution*, Penguin, Harmondsworth.

6

THE NATIONAL CURRICULUM – AN AGENDA FOR THE NINETIES

PETER R. WATKINS

*After teaching history for thirteen years at Bristol Grammar school,
Peter Watkins was appointed headteacher first of a grammar school,
then of a comprehensive (Chichester High School). After a period as
Principal of a Sixth Form College, Mr Watkins moved to the School
Curriculum Development Council as Deputy Chief Executive, a post
which he held from 1984 to 1988. He was then appointed Deputy Chief
Executive to the National Curriculum Council, finally resigning in
1991.*

*Below is the full text of the Raymond Priestley lecture Peter Watkins
delivered at the University of Birmingham School of Education on 14
November 1991.*

INTRODUCTION

When historians look back from the perspective of the twenty-first
century on education in the twentieth century I believe they will be
surprised, not that we introduced a national curriculum in 1989 but,
that for forty-five years between 1944 and 1989 we had no national
specification beyond the requirement to include religious education.
The curriculum was left entirely to heads and teachers with only
minimal involvement of LEAs and none at all of central government.
National prescription was a characteristic of most of the educational
systems of the world, of the French, the German and the Japanese, for
example, but it was, we believed, entirely unnecessary in England,

alien indeed to our liberal tradition.

Yet the school curriculum has not always been without specification. The Revised Code set out the elementary school curriculum from 1862-95, and was execrated by teachers because it was tied to payment by results. Prescription lingered on in attenuated form in elementary schools until 1926 and in secondary schools until 1944. The national curriculum set out in the Education Reform Act (1988) was therefore a reversion to an earlier period. Teachers, however, had been brought up in the postwar world and their reaction to its introduction was, not surprisingly, one of shock, resentment and even anger.

TWO ACHIEVEMENTS

Acceptance of the Principle of a National Curriculum
That has wholly changed. I want to make two propositions about the experience of the national curriculum since it was introduced into schools only two years ago. The first is the acceptance of the principle of a national curriculum by almost everybody involved in education. The truth of Kenneth Baker's remarks to the North of England Education Conference in January 1987 has been broadly acknowledged. 'It must be ridiculous,' he said, 'to leave 27,000 individual schools to make their own lonely decisions about curriculum and to defend themselves against a hostile environment. We shall all – teachers, parents, employers, pupils, teacher trainers – gain from having a broad specification of the curriculum which schools are following.' The case for a national curriculum in a state system of education seems to me unanswerable. It is indeed accepted to such an extent that the great majority of independent schools, though not obliged to follow it, have chosen to do so.

The National Curriculum is a Success
My second proposition is that the national curriculum is already a success. Standards in many schools are higher than they were. I want to say that loud and clear because both politicians and teachers tend to emphasise deficiencies and highlight problems when they ought to applaud success. Monitoring of the introduction of the national curriculum and early evaluation by HMI, NCC, LEAs and teacher associations have made clear some of the benefits which schools are already reaping. Let me give you four examples:

First, aspects of subjects previously undervalued are taking their place in the curriculum: speaking and listening in English, shape and space in mathematics, physical science and technology in primary schools, for example.

Second, there is a much better balance between knowledge, skills and understanding. We are at last realising that knowledge without skills and understanding to apply it, are of little use except perhaps to compete in 'Mastermind'. (It is a point our political masters are slow to grasp when they propose to test knowledge by means of 'pencil and paper' tests, separately from the accompanying skills and understanding.)

Third, the curriculum shows fewer signs of the gender bias whose effect was usually to discriminate against girls.

Fourth, the national curriculum has proved to be a catalyst for joint planning by heads and staffs in primary schools and by subject departments in secondary schools. Co-operation between all sorts of groupings of teachers is taking place to the benefit of their pupils. The national curriculum is at last bringing about curriculum continuity between primary and secondary schools. It is spelling the end of the teacher going it alone behind the closed door of the classroom.

The national curriculum is, then, an idea whose time has come, and it is to the credit of the politicians who introduced it to a chorus of disapproval that they recognised that. Its early success is, however, above all a tribute to the dedicated hard work of teachers at all levels. I wish that was said more often, particularly by politicians, including ministers.

THREE IMPLEMENTATION ISSUES

But of course, it is early days. Specification is nearing completion; implementation has only just begun (see Table 6.1). The last orders, those for art, music and physical education, were only published in spring 1992. This has completed a gestation period of almost five years from the summer of 1987 when the first working groups were set up.

Implementation is at a much earlier stage. I have invented a new piece of national curriculum jargon – a unit of implementation (see Table 6.2). If you exclude art and music at key stage 4 (likely to be optional), there are exactly one hundred units of implementation. Seventeen had been completed by the end of the 1991 academic year.

Table 6.1: Sequence of national curriculum subject working groups and statutory orders

Subject	Working group set up	Final report published	Order published
mathematics	July 1987	August 1988	March 1989 December 1991 (revised)
science	July 1987	August 1988	March 1989 December 1991 (revised)
English 5-11	April 1988	November 1988	May 1989
5-16		June 1989	March 1990
Welsh	April 1988	April 1989	May 1990
technology	April 1988	June 1989	March 1990
history	January 1989	July 1990	March 1991
geography	May 1989	June 1990	March 1991
modern foreign language	August 1989	October 1990	November 1991
art, music and physical education	July 1990	August 1991	March 1992

Note: in Welsh, history, geography, art and music there are separate statutory orders specifying curriculum in these subjects for schools in Wales.

Thirty-two, or just under one third, were completed in July 1992. In two crucial areas there is as yet no national curriculum requirement: years five and six in primary school and years ten and eleven, key stage 4, in secondary school. There is much still to be done.

It is nevertheless a good time to review the national curriculum. I want to suggest three implementation issues: time and overload, complexity and over-prescription, and key stage 4, all need urgent attention. I then turn to how these might be tackled and, in particular, what might be the role of the National Curriculum Council.

There is first one fundamental problem from which all others stem. The national curriculum had no architect, only builders. Many people were surprised at the lack of sophistication in the original model: ten subjects, attainment targets and programmes of study defined in a few words in the Bill, that was all. Indeed such design as there was seemed to be retrospective. The working groups for science and mathematics

Table 6.2: Introduction of national curriculum subjects by key stages and year groups

Key stage	1		2				3			4	
Year	1	2	3	4	5	6	7	8	9	10	11
mathematics	89	90	90	91	92	93	89	90	91	92	93
science	89	90	90	91	92	93	89	90	91	92	93
English	89	90	90	91	92	93	90	91	92	92	93
technology	90	91	90	91	92	93	90	91	92	93	94
history	91	92	91	92	93	94	91	92	93	94	95
geography	91	92	91	92	93	94	91	92	93	94	95
art	92	93	92	93	94	95	92	93	94		
music	92	93	92	93	94	95	92	93	94		
physical education	92	93	92	93	94	95	92	93	94	95	96
modern foreign languages							92	93	94	95	96

were set up before the Bill was published and reported before the Act was passed. The report of the Task Group on Assessment and Testing did not appear until the first working groups had produced their interim reports. The lack of a framework was pointed out by the School Curriculum Development Committee in its response to the consultation document, but to no effect.

Nor was there any consideration of resources – time, teachers, technology or buildings. No industrial enterprise (whose example the Government so often urges us to follow) would have embarked upon a major development without a full specification backed by the allocation of resources. To do so they know would lead at best to waste and avoidable changes of specification, and at worst it may jeopardise the whole enterprise.

Time and Overload
Let me turn, however, to specific issues. The first is whether the national curriculum can be delivered within the length of the school day and year. When the working groups were set up their chairpersons were provided with guidelines for the likely time allocation to the

subject at each key stage. The guidance was not offered to the last three groups nor is there any indication about the time which might be allocated to religious education. Reticence is perhaps understandable since the total was already uncomfortably close to 100 per cent (see Table 6.3).

Table 6.3: Notional time for national curriculum subjects

	Key stage 1		Key stage 2		Key stage 3		Key stage 4*	
mathematics	20		20		10		10	10
English	20		20		15		12.5	12.5
science	12.5		12.5		10	15	20	12.5
technology					5	10	5	5
history	7.5-10		7.5-10		7.5-10		10	5
geography	7.5-10		7.5-10		7.5-10			5
modern foreign languages					10		10	5-7.5
art	[7.5]		[6]		[5]			
music	[5]		[5]		[5]			
physical education	(5)		(5)		(5)		(5)	(5)
religious education	(5)		(5)		(5)		(5)	(5)
	90	95	89	94	85	100	77.5-	65

Percentages, apart from those in brackets, are drawn from supplementary guidance to the chairperson of the subject working groups.
( ) Notional.
[ ] Working group report based on present practice.
* Figures for key stage 4 are based on compulsory subjects only.
In supplementary guidance the Welsh working group was recommended to assume 20 per cent of curriculum time for Welsh in the primary phase in Welsh speaking schools. 'Elsewhere, it may be between 10 per cent and 12.5 per cent of total curriculum time, although it could be higher in schools where Welsh is given a greater emphasis.'

We do not know how the working groups used the guidelines to assess the amount they put into the programmes of study. They were all by definition specialists and enthusiasts for their subject and it is unlikely that they underestimated the amount which could and should be covered.

The view of many teachers who have begun to implement the orders is that quarts have been squeezed into pint pots. Primary teachers, who have not in the past had to allocate time to individual subjects, are asking how they can prune science and technology to accommodate history and geography and still ensure that the basic skills of reading, writing and arithmetic do not suffer. The problems of overload at key stage 4 have been rehearsed *ad nauseam*.

There are, of course, two solutions: contraction of content or expansion of time. Perhaps both will be needed. It has always seemed to me odd that the DES recommended difference in length of school day appropriate to an eight-year-old and a sixteen-year-old is six minutes a day (23.5 hours per week up to age eleven compared with 24 hours for twelve-to-sixteen-year-olds). Are our school days simply too short for what we want to achieve in them? Pupils in Japan certainly work significantly longer hours. So does the local City Technology College at Kingshurst. So too do many independent schools. The argument could be extended to the school year of 190 days. If we want higher standards, including a broader curriculum, we may simply need longer to achieve it. But let me stress not necessarily longer teaching time but longer learning time. There is much scope for exploiting modern technology in imaginative schemes of supported self-study by pupils.

Complexity and Overprescription

I take for the heading of my second implementation issue the phrase which has increasingly crept into ministerial statements of late – 'complexity and overprescription'. Is the national curriculum too complex and is it prescribed in too much detail? Does it inhibit innovative and imaginative teaching? Does it, by implication, prescribe method as well as content? The usual inference is that if it does, this is the fault of the NCC and the SEAC which have complicated what was meant to be simple. This is not the case. Both Councils have accepted ministerial directions about the degree of detail required. Indeed detailed specification was until recently seen as a virility test. It was, for example, thought by ministers and civil servants that geography would be more rigorous if it had five attainment targets instead of the three favoured by many in the NCC and by an amplitude of level statements.

The subject working groups upon whose recommendations the Secretary of State based the orders worked in isolation from one another and over a period of three years. There was no equivalent of GCSE general criteria. There were no detailed definitions of attainment targets and programmes of study, so their number and nature vary substantially. Let me give you three examples:

> Three subjects have attainment targets which are broadly process-based – English, modern foreign languages and technology. Three are content-led – science, mathematics and geography – while history is a hybrid.
>
> The number of level statements varies too. Science started with 407 but has been reduced to 173. History, however, has forty-five while geography now heads the list with 183.
>
> Programmes of study are provided in some subjects for each key stage, in some for each level, and in some for a combination of level and key stage.

These differences arise not from the nature of the subject but from the decisions of the working groups. How will teachers cope with the differences, particularly teachers in primary schools who will shortly have no less than nine ring-binders from which to work as they devise schemes of work and lesson plans?

The problems of complexity and overprescription might be tackled in a number of ways. First, it could be decided that a curriculum drawn up by nine working groups is not appropriate at key stage 1. What pupils aged five to seven need above all is to acquire mastery of the basic skills of reading, writing and arithmetic. There is plenty of evidence to show that later success or failure at school is directly related to early and complete acquisition of these skills. Material from the non-core foundation subjects needs to be drawn together into a unified curriculum for the key stage, devised to endorse and consolidate the basic skills.

Second, the programmes of study could be reduced so as to constitute a minimum statutory requirement. These could then be enhanced by teachers to meet the needs of pupils of varied abilities and aptitudes. Many people maintain that, for all but the ablest pupils, there is simply too much in the programmes of study, for example, for science and geography. History could be reduced to the core units, leaving schools discretion to add as much as they reasonably could.

Third, we might revert to what Mrs Thatcher is alleged to have wanted in the first place – a statutory curriculum consisting of the three core subjects. The attainment targets and programmes of study in the remaining foundation subjects would become non-statutory guidelines. There is every reason to believe schools would make good use of them. It is worth remembering that in Scotland there is no national curriculum yet the staying-on rate at sixteen is substantially higher than it is in England.

Fourth, it seems essential even at this late stage to put some architecture round the building. Is it to be Gothic, classical or modern, and can we eliminate some of the 'monstrous carbuncles'? To put it more prosaically we need a national curriculum criteria document which synthesises the separate instructions to the working groups and provides a framework for the whole curriculum. This would include a section on cross-curricular themes. It would give guidance on the number and nature of attainment targets and level statements, whether the programmes of study should be for a key stage or each level, and how much detail they should provide.

Key Stage 4

My final implementation issue is the vexed problem of key stage 4, the curriculum for the last two years of compulsory schooling. It is a paradigm of all the problems I have so far outlined, putting a quart if not a gallon into a pint pot. In fact, it is a case study of complexity and overprescription. One of the underlying principles of the national curriculum was that all pupils should have a broad, balanced curriculum to sixteen. No longer would it be possible for them to drop vital elements at thirteen or fourteen. They would all study balanced science and technology as well as a modern foreign language, history, geography and the creative arts, and also including religious and physical education. In addition there would be room for some but not many other subjects. The curriculum of pupils from fourteen to sixteen would be more demanding and more rigorous, and would require the study of more subjects than hitherto, but that was in line with the practice of other countries and it would keep open a variety of routes into education post-sixteen.

That was the vision; and perhaps it was always too idealistic to be realisable. During 1991, however, it came under attack from a number of quarters, and the vision has become a nightmare. The national curriculum is, to all intents and purposes, dead beyond the end of key stage 3. Let me list some of the pressures now being brought to bear on key stage 4.

First, the Secretary of State wants to see a vocational element included for at least some pupils, though harnessed to the national curriculum. It is not at all clear what this means. There is doubt about whether the sort of qualifications hitherto provided by the vocational examining bodies are appropriate for schools and whether they have the resources to offer them widely in any case. There is a danger that this could mark a return to an academic route for the able and a vocational route for the less able. Perhaps the test will be whether the independent sector offers vocational courses on any scale.

Second, pressure along similar lines was suggested recently by Granada Television's commission on education. It proposed channelling pupils at fourteen into one of three paths – academic, technical or vocational. This proposal too needs careful scrutiny. In the past all multi-track systems in England at whatever age have produced a hierarchy. Can we avoid it this time?

Third, concern is being exprssed about the nature of national curriculum technology. In trying to devise a new omnibus subject we may have produced an unwieldy monster stronger on design and evaluation than on traditional craft skills. National curriculum technology may even retard, rather than encourage, a vocational slant to the curriculum.

These three pressures are all concerned with the place of technological and vocational education for fourteen- to sixteen-year-olds.

The fourth pressure arises directly out of the national curriculum. Once it is accepted that not all national curriculum subjects will be compulsory beyond the age of fourteen, what is the educational rationale for deciding which are dispensable? Why are creative arts, and either geography or history, more dispensable under all circumstances for all pupils than a modern foreign language? Can you draw an educationally defensible line anywhere between the three core subjects and any of the other foundation subjects? And to complete the litany, what credibility will the proposed short courses in, for example, foreign languages or history have in the market place?

Behind these pressures I discern a deeper issue. We now have three competing models for a curriculum and assessment system at key stage 4. They overlap with one another but there are serious areas of incompatibility. It is this which we need to address rather than pretending that a little cosmetic surgery will solve the problem. The three models are:

GCSE is a norm-referenced examination which reports its results in subjects, using at present a seven point scale A-G, of which schools have valuable experience and in which they, as well as parents and employers, have confidence.

The national curriculum is a criterion-referenced system with accompanying assessment in attainment targets at ten levels each notionally representing two years progress. The extent of the incompatibility between national curriculum assessment at sixteen and GCSE is just being realised.

Vocational qualifications, at present used mostly beyond the age of sixteen, make extensive use of modules, coursework, credit accumulation and transfer.

I have perhaps said enough to suggest that the agenda of my title could be filled with key stage 4 issues alone.

REVIEWING THE NATIONAL CURRICULUM

I have argued so far that the national curriculum is both accepted in principle and a success in practice. I have, however, gone on to suggest that three years after the passing of the Education Reform Act serious problems are evident which need to be addressed. Let me turn now from the 'what' to the 'how' of national curriculum review.

No curriculum is static, nor should it be. It must be capable of undergoing review to meet deficiencies which become apparent in use and, in the longer term, to meet the changing needs of society. On the other hand, altering the curriculum is not like introducing a new railway timetable or adjusting the rules of football – something which causes only minor inconvenience to users or players. It is more like introducing new local government boundaries: it has wide repercussions. For teachers it is a substantial task to draw up new schemes of work and to resource them. A revised curriculum must be understood by parents, employers and others. It has consequences for examining bodies and publishers. You cannot change the curriculum just because there is a new Secretary of State (the average tenure since the war is just over two years), nor even because there is a new Prime Minister (where durability has been better, particularly during the last decade). Indeed, it would be a very serious matter if a change of Prime Minister, Secretary of State or politial party were to have a significant impact on the school curriculum. It must be altered only for real and agreed educational reasons.

It had been assumed that there would be no amendment to the national curriculum at least until all the subjects were in place and there was experience of how they were working in the classroom. In fact, this year there has already been a radical review of the attainment targets and level statements in science and mathematics, with smaller changes to the programmes of study. The English order may now be under the microscope. Some believe it is not sufficiently rigorous in its demand for knowledge about language, others, such as SEAC, are concerned that it will be difficult and expensive to assess at GCSE.

Before we go further down this road, deciding perhaps that geography needs to be simplified, we must surely have a strategy for review. Piecemeal and overhasty review can only undermine the credibility of the national curriculum, as well as making it impossible to implement in schools. Teachers must know that there is a rationale, a plan, a realistic timescale and that they will be consulted. In Japan, for instance, the curriculum runs on a ten-year-cycle with the process of revision beginning after five years.

THE NATIONAL CURRICULUM COUNCIL

Review of the national curriculum brings me to the role of the National Curriculum Council. The Council is the first national body there has ever been in England with a broad remit for the curriculum as a whole. You may be surprised that I should say this since the NCC had two predecessors, the Schools Council and the School Curriculum Development Committee. The Schools Council was set up in 1964, but with a self-denying ordinance. Its foundation document, the Lockwood Report, adopted as a fundamental principle 'that the schools should have the fullest possible measure of responsibility for their own work, including responsibility for their own curriculum and teaching methods which should be evolved by their own staff to meet the needs of their own pupils'. The School Curriculum Development Committee, whose brief existence followed the demise of the Schools Council, was, as its name makes clear, a curriculum development body not permitted to take an overview of curricular provision across the system.

The National Curriculum Council, set up under section 14 of the Education Reform Act is the Government's curriculum body, though chiefly an advisory rather than an executive body. It must work with the grain of government policy but offer independent advice. Equally, it must listen to the teaching profession and the wider education service without becoming their mouthpiece.

The NCC has now existed for three years and during that time it has gained an established place in the educational firmament. It has succeeded, I believe, in advising the Government and listening to the profession. Now, however, the independence of the Council and indeed that of the SEAC are in jeopardy. The Councils seem to be regarded by the Government not as sources of independent, authoritative advice but are used to endorse and set out in detail what the Secretary of State has already decided to do. If they decline to accept this role their advice is ignored, changed or rejected. It is, of course, unexceptionable in a parliamentary democracy that the Secretary of State should have the power to determine the curriculum for schools, subject to Parliament, just as the Secretary of State for Defence determines the size of the army or the Secretary of State for Health the framework of the national health service. It is, however, equally a constitutional principle that this power should be exercised over broad areas of policy leaving the details to professional advisers and should be exercised with restraint. The Secretary of State for Defence should not decide which aircraft to use in the Gulf, nor the Secretary of State for Health prescribe the drugs required to treat a particular illness.

Yet that is what is happening over the curriculum. The Council's advice on key stage 4 was ignored and a new framework announced without the Council even being informed, let alone consulted. It is the Secretary of State not his assessment adviser, the SEAC, who has decided the date when SATs will be administered at the end of key stage 3 in 1992. The Prime Minister has stepped in to announce a drastic reduction in the amount of coursework which will be permitted in GCSE. In so doing he has overthrown one of the fundamental principles of GCSE as approved by Lord Joseph. He shows no understanding why coursework is so important intrinsically and pedagogically, particularly for girls. He has ignored the importance of the motivation it provides for pupils throughout their two-year course and the evidence it offers of skills such as drafting and writing an extended essay which can be tested in no other way.

STATUTORY CONSULTATION

A central part of the role of the NCC is to carry out consultations under section 20 of the Education Reform Act. The Council has undertaken, or is in process of undertaking, no less than thirteen consultations (two on each core subject and one on each of the other foundation subjects). The machinery has worked reasonably well. Those consulted have felt they had a real opportunity to take part in the process and that their views were taken into consideration. Schools too, though not formally consulted, have welcomed the opportunity to contribute and have done so in large numbers.

The legislation clearly intended the Secretary of State normally to accept the Council's advice and only exceptionally to modify or reject it. In fact, he has increasingly taken his own stance on subjects, changing the Council's advice in ways which appear cavalier. The most flagrant example was his decision that national curriculum history should end twenty years ago – a decision criticised by university historians, teachers and others as quite indefensible. Significant changes were also made to the NCC's recommendations for geography.

The consultation procedure was designed for use when the Secretary of State introduces a new national curriculum subject or amends one already in place. It is much less satisfactory in what can be described as single issue consultations. The Council is currently consulting about the disapplication of art and music at key stage 4; about the proposal to make history and geography alternative also at key stage 4; about permitting whole classes to take GCSE early; and about special provision for the three sciences to be examined through GCSE in 1994.

In each case the Secretary of State has already announced his decision. Indeed, art and music proposals were actually published with the title 'Art for ages five to fourteen' and 'Music for ages five to fourteen' as though the issue were closed. What price consultation? A different procedure is needed. Either the Secretary of State should announce his decision and not be required to consult or he should couch his suggestions in a broader context, inviting the NCC to consult and make recommendations. He should then normally accept the Council's proposals.

CONCLUSIONS

The national curriculum is, I believe, the most significant innovation in the classroom since mass education began 120 years ago. It has got off to a good start. There is now, however, need for a full-scale review carried out urgently but to a realistic timescale. It must be undertaken in full co-operation with the teaching profession, the wider educational community and what are now called consumer interests (including parents, employers and higher education). The review needs to be initiated by the Secretary of State, but he should then distance himself from its detailed work. The enterprise is too important to be compromised by political partisanship or point-scoring by pressure groups. It is the government's curriculum body, the National Curriculum Council, which should be entrusted with the co-ordination of the review, and for advising the Government on subsequent action. Only if such a review takes place can the momentum already gained by the national curriculum be sustained and the raising of standards for which it was introduced be achieved.

7

THE NATIONAL CURRICULUM IN PRIMARY SCHOOLS: A DREAM AT CONCEPTION, A NIGHTMARE AT DELIVERY

JIM CAMPBELL

This is a revised and updated version of a lecture presented to the Education Section of the annual conference of the British Association for the Advancement of Science, held at Southampton University in August 1992. Jim Campbell is Professor of Education at the University of Warwick and author of Developing the Primary School Curriculum *(1985) and* Humanities in the Primary School *(1990). He is editor of* Education 3-13 *and national chair of the Association for the Study of Primary Education. The findings of his current research into the impact of the national curriculum upon teachers' work are to be published in three volumes by Routledge in 1993.*

INTRODUCTION

My argument in this paper is a threefold one. First, I shall try to show that the national curriculum *model*, as it was conceived, and as it has emerged over the period since 1987, offered the dream of substantial and much-needed improvement to curriculum practice in primary schools in England and Wales generally. Second, I believe that six assumptions were made about the *professional context* within which primary teachers were working, and five of these assumptions were so mistaken as to render the full delivery of the national curriculum impossible for normal teachers. The dream became, or is becoming, a nightmare. Third, I shall examine some ways forward, although all of them are contentious politically or professionally, and most have resource implications.

Perhaps I should express two notes of caution by way of introduction. The first is obvious. The national curriculum is not yet fully in place in its statutory form in any school at either key stage 1 or key stage 2. At key stage 1, the last three subjects – art, PE and music – apply in statutory form from the year 1992–93. At key stage 2, all nine (or ten in Wales) subjects will apply to all relevant years of pupils only in 1996 at the earliest, provided that we ignore the possibility of further revisions. Therefore, any declarations of the failure of the national curriculum could be construed as my writing its obituary prematurely, the pessimistic obverse of the assertions already made by Government Ministers and others, of its resounding and immediate success. So I would want to stress the tentativeness of the available research evidence, nearly all of which refers to key stage 1 only. Nevertheless, however tentative the evidence, we need to try to make sense of it quickly so as to feed it back into policy-making. I am assuming that the fundamental basic *curriculum model* of nine or ten subjects, plus RE, is established and will survive any modification of detail, though this may be questionable.

The second introductory point is more difficult to make briefly. Under the imposed reforms of the 1988 Act there has been a tendency among educationists to invent a 'golden age' of primary education in the past, whose destruction is being brought about by the reform process. The image of this golden age was derived from the Plowden Report (1967) in which rounded pictures were presented of good practice in a part of the report (para.277ff) where 'composite' schools were seen through the eyes of an 'imaginary visitor'. The image offered was concrete, detailed and suffused with light and joy, showing a school world of emotional security and well-being for pupils, combined with a range of artistic and cultural activity apparently unconstrained by time, or the pupils' age, or intellectual shortcomings among staff or pupils:

> The nursery class has its own quarters and the children are playing with sand, water, paint, clay, dolls, rocking horses and big, posh toys, under the supervision of their teacher. There is serenity in the room, belying the belief that happy children are always noisy . . . Learning is going on all the time but there is not much direct teaching.
>
> Going out into the playground the visitor finds a group of children with

their teacher, clustered round a large, square box full of earth. The excitement is all about an earthworm, which none of the children had ever seen before. Their classroom door opens onto the playground and inside are the rest of the class, seated at tables disposed informally about the room, some reading books that they themselves have chosen from the copious shelves along the side of the room, and some measuring the quantities of water that different vessels will hold. Soon the teacher and worm-watchers return, except for two children who have gone to the library to find a book on worms, and the class begins to tidy up in preparation for lunch. The visitor's attention is attracted by the paintings on the wall, and as he looks at them he is soon joined by a number of children who volunteer information about them. In a moment the preparations for lunch are interrupted as the children press forward with things they have painted, or written, or constructed, to show them to the visitor . . . The sound of the music from the hall attracts the visitor and there he finds a class who are making up and performing a dance drama in which the forces of good are overcoming the forces of evil, to the accompaniment of drums and tambourines.

As he leaves the school and turns from the playground into the grubby and unlovely street on which it abuts, the visitor passes a class who, seated on boxes in a quiet, sunny corner, are listening to their teacher telling them the story of Rumpelstiltskin.

On this reading of the history of post war primary education, children's spontaneity, creativity and curiosity are being killed off in the name of curriculum reform. As a picture of practice it is a fiction. The evidence from HMI surveys (e.g., DES, 1978; 1982; 1985b) and academic research (e.g., Alexander, 1984; 1992; Bennett, 1976; Galton and Simon, 1980; Barker-Lunn, 1982; 1984; Bealing, 1972) about the national picture of curriculum practice and pedagogy in primary schools in the twenty-odd years before the Education Reform Act, revealed not so much a golden as a rather leaden age. The curriculum was narrow, emphasising literacy and numeracy through repetitive exercises; despite encouragement, work in science was patchy and haphazard; standards in the social subjects were lower than might be expected; pedagogy was often characterised by an undifferentiated focus on the pupils in the middle levels of attainment within a class, and expectations of the able children were undemanding. Continuity and progression in curriculum experience had remained elusive, and assessment and record-keeping, other than in the basic skills of reading and number, were rarely systematic. Plowdenesque progressivism flowered largely in rhetoric, with progressive practice, however defined, being a minority taste amongst the teachers.

I said it was difficult to make the point briefly, and one reason is that a two-minute survey of the evidence comes out sounding suspiciously like teacher-bashing. But this would be an almost entirely wrong interpretation. The real problem lay in the absence of anything approaching a public policy for the primary curriculum before 1988. The primary teachers, as much as anyone else, were the victims of this policy vacuum and not its creators.

What the 1988 Act introduced was a policy framework for the curriculum that had been previously lacking in primary education.

THE CHARACTER OF THE DREAM

There were five features of the proposed national curriculum that proved seductive to most of those working in primary education.

First, there was the concept of *entitlement*. Articulated most clearly in the House of Commons 3rd Report (House of Commons, 1986), a national curriculum would provide a legal framework of common entitlement for children that would remove the inconsistencies of curricular provision, (see Richards, 1982), which had arisen arbitrarily from class teacher autonomy. For the first time since 1944 pupils and parents would be able to know what the school should provide in curriculum terms, as would the school staff and governors. In effect, the notion of entitlement promised greater equality of curricular experience for children.

Second, and linked to the concept of entitlement, was the promise of real *breadth and balance*. A statutory curriculum in which *all* foundation subjects, not just the core, would be allocated reasonable amounts of time and emphasis, seemed to offer a once-and-for-all opportunity to destroy the elementary approach to curriculum with its narrow concentration on basic skills. The 1988 Education Act required a 'balanced and broadly based' curriculum, and the DES Circular 5/89 emphasised breadth and balance (p17) requiring, from August 1989, that each of the core and foundation subjects should be allocated 'reasonable' time for worthwhile study.

Third, included in the legal definition of the curriculum, was a set of *assessment arrangements* which would require a radical rethinking not merely of assessment but also of teaching itself. The TGAT report (DES, 1988) was sold to the profession by its emphasis on the formative purposes of assessment. Before 1988 most assessment in primary schools had employed narrowly focused tests of reading comprehension and number, predominantly at the end of the infant and junior stages, (see Gipps, 1988; 1990). Under the TGAT proposals the emphasis would shift to continuous assessment, involving the diagnosis of individual pupils' needs through observing them learning, talking with them about their learning and using the observations for planning the next steps in learning.

Fourth, it was a *modernising* curriculum. It was not merely that science was included in the core but that the kind of science involved acknowledged advances in physics, biology and chemistry; technology, including information technology, was in the foundation; mathematics included the handling of data, and most other subjects called for applications using computers. English called for literature that was global. The national curriculum was, in effect, an attempt to haul the primary curriculum towards a state of knowledge and information processing relevant to the latter decade of the twentieth century.

Finally, there was the relationship of the curriculum to *standards*. Primary education in England and Wales had been characterised by relatively low standards, especially in relation to children judged to be able (DES, 1978; 1990b; Alexander *et al.*, 1992). The common and possibly facile explanation for this state of affairs was that teacher expectations were too low, especially in inner cities and other areas of poverty. Following a series of important observational studies at Exeter University (Bennett *et al.*, 1984; Bennett and Dunne, 1992; Bennett, 1991; 1992), the demonstration of poor match between tasks set by teachers and pupil capacities (or, to be precise, sometimes poor pupil understanding of the task) lent force to the argument that the national curriculum was intended to raise standards in two ways. First, expectations of able children would be raised through the explicitly differentiated levels in which the attainment targets were specified. Able children at the end of key stage 1 would be operating at levels 3 or 4, and at the end of key stage 2 at levels 5 or 6. Second, standards would be raised simply by virtue of teaching being planned, delivered and assessed according to systematic programmes of study and set targets right *across* the nine subject areas. Standards would no longer be defined narrowly by reference to standards in English and mathematics.

Thus the promotion of the national curriculum held out the promise of a transformation of curriculum practice in primary schools. As a conception of the curriculum for contemporary primary schools at the end of the twentieth century it looked like a dream package.

CRITICAL PERSPECTIVES

Six Preconditions for Effective Implementation

There are problems with the model, but the criticism I am advancing here is not focused on the curriculum model itself but on what appear to be six assumptions about the *professional contexts* of primary schools; they are assumptions, to to speak, about the bed into which the national curriculum was to be delivered. They are the preconditions that needed to be met if the dream was to become a reality. The six assumptions are as follows:

1. Primary teachers would approve of, and commit themselves to, the national curriculum.

2. There would be adequate curricular expertise in the primary teaching force and, if not, that it could be provided through in-service training.

3. There would be available to every school adequate curricular expertise to deliver the national curriculum, mainly through its own staffing deployment.

4. Most class teachers in primary schools would have the curricular expertise and pedagogical skills to deliver and assess, with some limited support, a curriculum in nine subjects and RE, appropriately differentiated according to the levels of the national curriculum statements of attainment.

5. Delivering the national curriculum would not increase or intensify teachers' term-time workloads beyond what was sustainable or reasonable.

6. There would be adequate time in the school day/week/term/year to meet the 'reasonable time' expectation for all the foundation subjects and RE.

These assumptions are not the stuff of curriculum theory – they are mundane considerations – but they are of great practical significance to those charged with delivering the curriculum. My reading of the early evidence is that only the first assumption turned out to be correct; all the others are beginning to look mistaken.

DELIVERING THE NATIONAL CURRICULUM: THE EMERGING NIGHTMARE

The evidence about what it has been like to be delivering the national curriculum is, in 1992, patchy and suggestive rather than comprehensive and certain, not least because the published evidence relates to the introduction of the statutory orders for the core subjects only. We do not know what the picture will look like for the delivery of the full national curriculum and RE. There are surveys by HMI (DES, 1989a; 1989b; 1990a; 1991a) and research reports on the early implementation stages (Campbell and Neill, 1990; Silcock, 1990; Campbell *et al.*, 1991; Coopers and Lybrand Deloitte, 1991; Core Subjects Association, 1991; NUT, 1991; Osborn and Pollard, 1991; Osborn and Broadfoot, 1991: Taylor and Stanley, 1991; Acker, 1992; Muschamp *et al.*, 1992; NCC, 1992).

TEACHER COMMITMENT TO THE NATIONAL CURRICULUM

It has become clear that teachers at key stage 1 in general approve of the national curriculum, and have been attempting to implement it. There is no evidence of serious subversion or of refusal to implement. On the contrary, studies at Bristol and Warwick Universities (Muschamp *et al.*, 1992; Osborn and Pollard, 1991; Campbell *et al.*, 1991) show the teachers supporting the principle, and objecting primarily to the pace, of the reforms. Moreover, the studies reveal that the teachers saw their professional skills as having been improved by implementing the national curriculum, especially their skills in planning, in whole school collaboration, and even in assessing children's progress. The Bristol team reported (Osborn and Pollard, 1991: 4) that some teachers spoke of the 'positive effect of having a structure and guidelines to work within' and that many felt that 'the emphasis that the national curriculum placed on reviewing and reflecting on their practice, and on having to read more widely and to collaborate more closely with other teachers, was an enhancement of their professionalism.' Likewise teachers in our study (Campbell *et al.*, 1991) spoke of the way they had been helped to become better teachers because of the need to plan and assess more systematically than hitherto. The findings from these research projects were supported generally in the survey reports by HMI (DES, 1989a; 1989b; 1990a) and by other surveys, such as the Core Subjects Association survey (CSA, 1991).

Moreover, with regard to science in primary schools there had been substantial improvement over previous practice, with the science curriculum now being planned and delivered in a more sustained and systematic way. This was an important achievement, given the constraints within which teachers were operating.

Thus the evidence about the first of the six assumptions is all in the same direction: infant teachers welcome and support the national curriculum and, far from being de-skilled by it, have found the process of implementing it improving their repertoire of professional skills. It is perhaps recognition of this view that has turned the initial opposition of teacher unions into motions of support at their annual conferences.

However, the evidence with regard to the other five assumptions provides less good news for those who want to see the reforms work; it suggests that, for class teachers, delivering the national curriculum has become, or will become, not a dream but a nightmare. It is simply not manageable even for experienced and able teachers. The reasons for believing this are different at key stage 1 and key stage 2, mainly because the empirical evidence refers to the former only. Therefore, rather than deal with the evidence on an assumption by assumption basis, I shall consider the emerging issues separately for each key stage.

Key Stage 1

At key stage 1 there appear to be four clusters of difficulties. First, our research projects at Warwick University (Campbell and Neill, 1990; Campbell *et al.*, 1991) have provided evidence about two aspects of teachers' workloads. We call them the *extensiveness* and the *intensiveness* of primary teaching. Extensiveness refers to the number of hours worked per term-time week, whereas intensiveness refers to the pressure during the working day. Our research showed conscientious teachers committed to implementing the national curriculum but having to work what the teachers considered unreasonably long hours. These varied but the average was about fifty-four hours a week, with one in five working a sixty hour week or more. Only about a third of this time was taken up with teaching, since the majority of their time was spent on non-teaching activities, such as preparation, marking, meetings, administration, in-service training and other professional development. Second, long hours were combined with intense pressure during the school day, with lack of time seen as the major obstacle to implementing the national curriculum. One teacher caught the perceptions of most others by her use of the metaphor of a 'running commentary':

> Well, what is frightening now is that we are being blinkered now into the national curriculum ... I am noticing it far more now that I never complete what I hope to achieve. There is always, like, a carry-forward so that you never get the feeling at the end of a session or day, 'Great, I've done this that I hoped we would do' ... there is this running commentary, really, in the background saying that, 'You haven't done this' or 'You haven't done that', which I find very annoying considering that you work so hard. (Campbell *et al*, 1991: para.2.14)

Delivering the curriculum was seen as an enervating treadmill in which the teachers worked very hard but obtained little sense of achievement. Not all of the workload was attributable directly to the national curriculum, but the overload had carried over into their personal and domestic lives, and most of the teachers were experiencing stress. The PACE project at Bristol (Osborn and Pollard, 1991; Osborn and Broadfoot, 1991) and the survey from the Core Subjects Association (CSA, 1991) came out with similar findings.

Second, and despite all this, the broad and balanced curriculum was not being delivered. Our 1991 evidence (Campbell *et al*, 1991) showed that the three core subject were taking, on average, at least half the timetabled time and that, at the very most, about fifteen minutes a day were left for each of the other foundation subjects and RE. Most of these subjects at key stage 1 are practical, time-consuming activities, such as art, PE, music and technology, and fifteen minutes per day (seventy-five minutes a week) seems inadequate for worthwhile treatment. I should add that for technical reasons concerning how time was recorded, the figure of fifteen minutes a day per subject is almost certainly an overstatement. The core was squeezing out the other parts of the basic curriculum. This view was supported by Muschamp *et al*. (1992).

We have some new data from our cohort in 1992. Tables 7.1 and 7.2 show these data. In our 1992 sample, teachers were asked to indicate which of the core and foundation subjects and RE they thought they had been able to devote adequate time to in their class in 1992. They were able to indicate all subjects, or none, or as many as reflected their perception. Ninety-seven teachers replied, so that if they all thought that all the subjects had received adequate time there would have been

970 responses; if they thought that none of the subjects had had adequate time there would have been no responses. As can be seen from Table 7.1, there was 477 responses, suggesting that the teachers overall saw only about half of the curriculum as having had adequate time devoted to it.

Table 7.1 Perceived adequacy of time devoted to subjects in key stage 1 teachers' classes 1992 (n = 97)

Subject	(a) No. of responses	(b) % of responses	(c) % of Teachers
English	79	16.6	81.4
mathematics	74	15.5	76.3
science	63	13.2	64.9
PE	58	12.2	59.8
art	49	10.3	50.5
technology	34	7.1	35.1
RE	34	7.1	35.1
music	31	6.5	32.0
geography	28	5.9	28.9
history	27	5.7	27.8
Total	477	100	n.a.

More detailed examination of column (c) in Table 7.1 reveals the teachers' perceptions about individual subjects. In this column the figures are the percentage of teachers thinking that the particular subject had had adequate time devoted to it in the current school year.

The differences in perceptions about different subjects are quite striking, given that, following DES Circular 5/89, from August 1989 all subjects were expected to have 'reasonable' time given to them. Teacher perceptions of what is adequate are not necessarily the only view of adequacy, of course, but their views are most important since they are the people responsible for the process of delivery.

We can treat the evidence in two ways, strictly and generously. On a strict view we might say that, where less than two thirds of the teachers thought a subject had adequate time, there is a *prima facie* case for saying that there is a problem. On the generous treatment we might say that, where less than half the teachers thought a subject has had adequate time, there is a problem. On the first assumption, only mathematics and English, in the view of these teachers, had had adequate time in 1992; on the second assumption, English, mathematics, science, PE and art had had adequate time. On either assumption the same five of the ten subjects were seen as having had inadequate time. These were technology, RE, music, and especially geography and history. The latter two subjects came bottom of the pile with fewer than three teachers in ten thinking that the time devoted to them was adequate.

We were able to set Table 7.1 against actual time given to the subjects in spring/summer 1992. This is given in Table 7.2:

Table 7.2: *Teaching time by curriculum subjects*

Subject	(a) Hours per week	(b) % of total time	(c) % of sum of column (a)
English	10.8	60	29
mathematics	6.7	34	18
science	3.5	19	9
art	3.3	18	9
technology	2.6	14	7
PE	1.3	7	4
geography	0.9	5	2
history	0.9	5	2
RE	0.5	3	2
Music	0.5	3	1
SATs	2.5	14	7
teacher assessment	1.7	9	5
other teaching	1.1	6	3
Total time spent teaching	18.0	100	100

Sum of individual subjects = 37.5 hours

Two findings from Table 7.2 are worth particular comment. There is an interesting and highly significant match between the order of subjects in this table and that in Table 7.1 above, which showed teachers' perceptions of the adequacy of time for particular subjects. If we exclude technology, the 'top' five subjects are identical and in almost identical order. Using the generous definition (more than 50 per cent of teachers thought the time was adequate) of adequacy above, our evidence is that the teachers perceived English, mathematics, science, art and PE as having adequate time given to them and that they had actually given most time to them. The teachers perceived geography, history, RE, music and technology as having had inadequate time and, except for technology, gave the least time to them. The relatively high position of Technology in Table 7.2 and its low position in Table 7.1 might be explained by the fact that it normally requires time-consuming, practical investigations, often using computers, and the time recorded, though relatively large, is still seen as inadequate. It should be remembered that in 1992 the statutory orders applied in the core and in history, geography and technology, but not in art, PE and music.

I am not suggesting that each subject needs the same amount of time for worthwhile delivery, merely that, when teachers' perceptions of inadequacy match a record of relatively low time actually spent, it is a reasonable hypothesis that the balanced and broadly based curriculum is not being delivered.

Second, there was a heavy concentration upon the core subjects. There are two ways of calculating this time. The simple one is to note what proportion of the eighteen hours given over to teaching was spent on each of the core subjects. This is given in column (b) of Table 7.2, which shows 60 per cent, 34 per cent and 19 per cent of total time given to English, mathematics and science respectively. (The percentages exceed 100 because teachers often taught two or more subjects simultaneously.) The more complex analysis is to take the sum of time spent on the different subjects, (*viz.* 37.5 hours), and express the time spent on each as a percentage of this sum. This is done in column (c) using rounded percentages. On this analysis, 56 per cent of teaching time was given over to the core, only 30 per cent was given over to the other foundation subjects, RE and other subjects, and 12 per cent was given over to teacher assessment and SATs. Since all SAT-time and most teacher assessment was focused on the core subjects, the 30 per cent figure for the non-core proportion is unlikely to be an underestimate. We think, irrespective of which analysis is used, that these findings show the core to be dominating the curriculum and that, for this reaason, the other foundation subjects and RE are being squeezed out.

The third point about key stage 1 is that, paradoxically, teachers claimed to be spending less time hearing children read in order to cover the new subjects, such as technology, and to manage assessment. This was also reported in Alexander *et al.* (1992). Another class management strategy reported by our teachers was setting most pupils time-consuming, low-level tasks to keep them occupied, to free up teachers to enable them to concentrate on assessing small groups of pupils or individuals. The irony here was that standards might be being lowered as part of teachers' attempts to meet what they saw as the assessment arrangements. This problem might have been exacerbated by the practice of 'multiple focus teaching', where teachers organised their classes so as to enable pupils to learn in integrated ways through topics covering several subjects, or for groups of pupils within a class to learn different subjects. We called this practice 'curriculum complexity', and the key stage 1 teachers in our research had much more complexity in their curricular organisation than those at key stage 2. The more complex the class organisation the more time-consuming planning, assessing and recording are likely to become.

Fourth, the formative purposes of assessment had been subverted by the pressure to provide accurate and fair end-of-key stage results for summative purposes. Teachers' confusion over the expectations for assessment and record-keeping was allied to a fear – I would say a paranoia – that sooner or later someone, probably inspectors, would be coming to check up on their records. We called this the 'key stage cops' syndrome. It had led to the teachers abandoning formative perspectives in fearful and frantic attempts to get summative results 'right', whatever that meant. HMI (DES, 1991b) found something similar when they reported teachers engaging in 'fervent but unfocused' assessment and recording. The publication of LEA 'league tables' towards the end of 1991 did little to allay the pressure on teachers to concentrate on the summative.

The picture emerging from our research was supported, or not contradicted, by other early studies (e.g., DES, 1991b; Taylor and Stanley, 1991; Smithers and Zientek, 1991; Coopers and Lybrand Deloitte, 1991). It shows, despite the commitment of hard-pressed teachers, that the curriculum at key stage 1 in 1990, 1991 and 1992 had few of the features of the dream package: it was not providing the entitlement to breadth and balance; assessment was not integrated diagnostically into teaching; and if it was being modernised through science and technology it might be at the expense of the rate of progress in pupils' achievement in reading.

Key Stage 2

The argument about unmanageability at key stage 2 is based on task analysis rather than empirical evidence since little of the latter is yet available. There are three elements here: the nature of the task facing the teacher; the expertise in the system; and the support available. Part of the problem is that the working groups based their recommendations for statutory orders on the best practice in their subject. This is

Table 7.3: *National curriculum at key stage 2 (September 1992)*

	No. of ATs	No. of statements of attainment	Level range
English	5	74	2 – 5
mathematics	5	83	2 – 6
science	4	64	2 – 5
technology	5	72	2 – 5
history	3	20	2 – 5
geography	5	80	2 – 5
PE	2	6	End of KS statement only:
art	2	7	End of KS statement only:
music	2	8	End of KS statement only:
Total	33	414	

understandable but the consequence for class teachers was horrific. They had, by law, to develop best practice in all subjects not just one. They had to become the primary school equivalent of Einstein, Madame Curie and Linford Christie rolled into one. Even in a slimmed-down version of the national curriculum, class teachers have over 400 statements of attainment to manipulate, detailed and confusingly presented programmes of study, poorly defined cross-curricular themes and religious education. In years five and six, the range of performance in a class is expected to be from probably level 2 to level 5 or 6 in each of the nine subjects of the national curriculum (see Table 7.3).

In small schools the range may be greater. The intellectual tasks demanded of class teachers are realisable only by Renaissance men and women. In this perspective, the assertion (Alexander *et al*., 1992) that 'Teachers must possess the subject knowledge which the statutory orders require', (para.120), begins to sound like a plea of desperation.

Second, there are few Renaissance men and women in the primary teaching force. The Primary Staffing Survey (DES, 1987) found fewer teachers qualified as main subject mathematics teachers than there were schools and, even using the most generous definition of qualification, only 400 teachers in the system qualified in technology. The study by Bennett and his colleagues (1992) showed serious problems of perceived competence and confidence to teach and assess many foundation subjects, especially technology. Evidence about low standards in a number of the subjects such as history and geography, (e.g., DES, 1978; DES, 1990), and in activities set in art lessons (e.g., Alexander, 1992) should not lead us to be sanguine about confidence and competence in the non-core subjects.

Third, the infrastructure of support in the LEAs for in-service training that might have helped bridge some of the gap between the task demands and the competencies of the teachers is being eroded (see Keep, 1992, for a fuller analysis). Schools may be being turned into small business, but one characteristic of small businesses is that they are not good at training their employees. Thus, class teachers at key stage 2, and especially in the latter two years of it, are facing statutory obligations that they cannot meet, even with high levels of commitment and effort, because hardly any individual teacher has the range and depth of knowledge required. In years five and six the class teacher's task of delivering the broad, balanced and differentiated curriculum looks dramatically impossible.

SIX WAYS FORWARD

This nightmare for primary teachers has been recognised obliquely, at least for those working in key stage 2 (Alexander *et al.*, 1992). I acknowledge the point made by Alexander *et al.* that no single solution will answer the problems of all schools, because of the diversity of schools in the system. Six possible ways forward seem worth exploring, though they are all controversial. And I am not for one moment suggesting that the resources required by some of them will be found, but I am advancing them because manageability is now the key issue in my view.

The first, in Alexander *et al* (1992), is that there should be greater flexibility in staff roles, with greater use of specialist, semi-specialist and co-ordinator roles, especially at the top end of key stage 2. This would make more use of existing curricular expertise within a staff group, by deploying teachers more frequently than at present, as specialists or semi-specialists teaching their subject to several classes. This is not a new idea: something similar was raised in the Plowden Report in 1967, discussed in the Primary Survey of 1978, and fully examined in the House of Commons Select Committee report in 1986. The problem with this idea is that subject co-ordinator roles were developed in some schools with great difficulty but limited success, given the lack of non-contact time, (see Campbell, 1985; 1988). The extensive use of specialist or semi-specialist teaching, would be difficult to adopt for the typical primary school of seven teachers, except where teachers have more non-contact time. In any case, for the one in five small schools (with ninety or fewer pupils) in the system, the options for exchanging specialisms are extremely circumscribed.

A second solution is to improve staffing levels in primary schools by the use of activity-led staffing models (Simpson, 1988; 1990) so as to fit staffing in primary schools to the tasks now required of them. Where this has been modelled (Kelly, 1991) it tended to equalise staffing across the five to sixteen age range. The problem here is that decisions about staffing have been devolved to schools, and the only way forward would be to develop a central policy to improve primary staffing through the funding formulae in the LMS schemes. These require approval from the Secretary of State so, in theory, it would deliver what is needed. However, its implementation, which would require central intervention in how teachers are deployed, perhaps along Section 11 lines, would run directly counter to the principle of devolved management and is unlikely to be attractive to DFE policy-makers or headteachers. In any case, it is unclear whether improved staffing levels in themselves can help with the problems of expertise in the primary teaching force as a whole, or with the task demands facing most class teachers, even after some specialist support has been provided.

The third solution is about the management of primary teachers' time. Our research showed that primary teachers typically spent between five and six hours a week on low-level routine activities – for example, registration, moving pupils around the school, supervising them, putting up displays, and attending school assemblies. All of these activities are very important from the point of view of socialising pupils, but not all of them need to be done by graduate teachers. More extensive use of non-teaching assistants might help free up teacher-time in the school day to engage in planning, recording and marking, whether jointly or as individuals. There is something odd about teachers spending five hours a week on these kinds of activities and at the same time saying that their main problem in achieving instructional objectives is lack of time. The idea of dividing labour in this way will probably be unattractive in the collaborative cultures of primary schools, but the use of para-professionals to support professionals is common in other countries.

The fourth solution is to modify the demands of the national curriculum so as to make them realisable for the majority of class teachers. There are two approaches here: the *radical* and the *ameliorative*. The former position (e.g., Oliver, 1984; Wicksteed, 1987) assumes that the broad and balanced curriculum is undeliverable and that a less broadly conceived approach would be more realistic. Whatever its attractions to those in the elementary tradition, this radical option seems politically impossible. The Conservative Government has committed itself to nine subjects and asserted that standards will rise across all of them. To change course now would be dramatically to demoralise teachers: it would be the curricular equivalent of leaving the ERM. The ameliorative position is that the teachers' task will become more reasonable if some major tidying-up of the existing curriculum were to be undertaken. Overlapping and inessential material could be excised, a standard format for all subjects introduced, and a less-detailed specification of curriculum items put in place. The revision of the mathematics and science orders for 1993 has led the way; other subjects could follow. This approach would help teachers, particularly with their use of documents for planning, but would still leave substantial problems of curricular expertise for most teachers.

The fifth solution would be to recognise that the 'multiple subject' approach to curriculum organisation through integrated topic work, or through group work based on different subjects going on simultaneously in classrooms, whatever its advantages in an ideal world, makes the task of delivering the national curriculum more difficult and time-consuming than is reasonable for most teachers. Planning of the curriculum might concentrate more often, or more typically, upon single subjects. There need be, as Alexander *et al.* (1992) point out, no loss of learning methods that use enquiry, firsthand experience, and independent sources, nor need the amount of group work be reduced. But the focus would be upon single subjects, or cognate subjects. The problem with this solution is that it ignores the fact that one reason why topic approaches are so popular is that they enable teachers to cover several areas in a short time, to be economical with curricular time. To separate them out will make visible the problem of content overload.

The sixth solution would be for schools to continue to rely upon the class teacher model but to introduce standard texts, learning materials or schemes in all, or most, subjects, in which the intellectual content would be provided for teachers, together with examples of learning and assessment tasks in differentiated levels. The advantage here is that the teachers could have a reasonable degree of confidence that the intellectual demands were appropriate in those areas where their own intellectual background was shaky. There will be understandable opposition to such a move from two quarters. First, there are those who believe that 'good practice' cannot be based on class texts in which learning tasks are fairly standard and progressively sequenced. Yet mathematics schemes of work, and reading schemes, are very close to such a format and are widely adopted.

The second source of opposition would be from those who fear state-prescribed texts and welcome its prohibition in the Education Reform Act 1988. Although these are common in other systems it could be argued that there is no reason for state approval in our system. Market forces are already operating and the emergence of new schemes and texts tailored to the current national curriculum requirements are emerging. Schools should have choice, assuming they have access to the kind of information needed to make it. This last point is problematic, especially at a time when specialist advice from LEA advisers and inspectors is being dismantled. State approval, rather like a British Standard, of any text or scheme that meets national curriculum criteria – though not state prescription of one official text – might be necessary.

The major problem here is in the culture of many primary schools, where teachers have been made to feel guilty about widespread use of class texts because they do not appear to meet the developmentalists' conceptions of 'good practice' where firsthand experience is at a premium.

The six solutions are not mutually exclusive. In some combination they could go a long way towards protecting the dream of the entitlement curriculum, and simultaneously making it realisable without subjecting teachers to the continuation of unmanageable workloads and a growing sense of failure. However, all but numbers four or five have resource implications, and all are, in this sense, political. But it is worth reiterating the point, made explicit in the Coopers and Lybrand Deloitte (1991) study, that implementing the national curriculum in primary schools carries substantial cost implications, both in materials and in staffing levels. To assume that it does not *is* to live in a dream world.

REFERENCES

Acker, S. (1991), 'Teacher Relationships and Educational Reform in England and Wales', *The Curriculum Journal*, vol.2, no.3.

Alexander, R. (1984), *Primary Teaching*, Holt Rinehart and Winston, London.

Alexander, R. (1992), *Policy and Practice in Primary Education*, Routledge, London.

Alexander, R., Rose, J. and Woodhead, C. (1992), *Curriculum, Organisation and Classroom Practice in Primary Schools: A Discussion Paper*, DES, HMSO, London.

Barker-Lunn (1982), 'Junior Schools and Their Organisational Policies', *Educational Research*, vol.24, no.4.

Barker-Lunn (1984), 'Junior Schoolteachers and their Methods and Practices', *Educational Research*, vol.26, no.3.

Bealing, D. (1972), 'The Organisation of Junior School Classrooms', *Educational Research*, vol.14, no.3.

Bennett, S.N. (1976), *Teaching Styles and Pupil Progress*, Open Books, London.

Bennett, S.N., Desforges, C., Cockburn, A. and Wilkinson, B. (1984), *The Quality of Pupil Learning Experiences*, Lawrence Erlbaum, New York.

Bennett, S.N. (1991), *Group Work*, Routledge, London.

Bennett, S.N. (1992), *Managing Learning in the Primary Classrooms*, ASPE Paper No.1, Trentham Books, Stoke.

Bennett, S.N. and Dunne, E. (1992), *Managing Classroom Groups*, Simon and Schuster, New York.

Campbell, R.J. (1985), *Developing the Primary School Curriculum*, Holt Rinehart and Winston, London.

Campbell, R.J. (1988), *Cashmore School*, Block ED.352, Open University Press, Milton Keynes.

Campbell, R.J. and Neill, S.R.StJ., (1990), *1330 Days*, Assistant Masters and Mistresses Association, London.

Campbell, R.J., Evans, L., Neill, S.R.StJ. and Packwood, S. (1991), *Workloads, Achievement and Stress*, Assistant Masters and Mistresses Association, London.

Coopers and Lybrand Deloitte (1991), *Costs of the National Curriculum in Primary Schools*, National Union of Teachers, London.

Core Subjects Association (1991), *Monitoring the Implementation of the National Curriculum*, NATE, Sheffield.

DES (1987), *Primary Education in England: A Survey by HMI*, HMSO, London.

DES (1982), *Education 5-9: An Illustrative Survey*, HMSO, London.

DES (1985b), *Education 8-12 in Middle and Combined Schools*, HMSO, London.

DES (1988), *Task Group on Assessment and Testing: A Report*, HMSO, London.

DES (1989a; 1989b; 1990a), series of reports called *The Implementation of the National Curriculum in Primary Schools*, Summer 1989, Autumn 1989, Summer 1990, London.

DES (1989c), *Circular 5/89*, HMSO, London.

DES (1990b), *Standards in Education 1988-90: Annual Report of HM Senior Chief Inspector of Schools*, HMSO, London.

DES (1991a), *The Implementation of the Curricular Requirements of ERA: An Overview by HM Inspectorate of the First Year*, HMSO, London.

DES (1991b), *Assessment, Recording and Reporting: A Report by HMI on the First Year, 1989-90*, HMSO, London.

Galton, M. and Simon, B. (1980), *Inside the Primary Classroom*, Routledge and Kegan Paul, London.

Gipps, C. (1988), 'The Debate over Standards and the Uses of Testing', *British Journal of Educational Studies*, vol.XXXVI, no.1, pp21-37.

Gipps, C. (1990), *Assessment: A Teacher's Guide*, Hodder and Stoughton, London.

House of Commons (1986), *ESAC 3rd Report: Achievement in Primary Schools*, vol.1, HMSO, London.

Keep, E. (1992), 'The Need for a Revised Management System for the Teaching Profession', *National Commission on Education*, Briefing No.2.

Kelly, A. (1991), 'Toward Objective Funding: An Activity-led Model of Teacher Staffing in Primary and Secondary Schools', British Educational Research Association, Annual Conference, Nottingham.

Muschamp, Y., Pollard, A. and Sharpe, R. (1992), 'Curriculum Management in Primary Schools', Bristol Polytechnic.

National Curriculum Council (1992), *Regional Primary Seminars: Report to Delegates*, NCC, York.

National Union of Teachers (1991), *'Miss, the Rabbit Ate the Floating Apple': The Case Against SATs*, NUT, London.

Oliver, D. (1984), 'Is Primary Education Possible?', *Education 3-13*, vol.12, no.2.

Osborn, M. and Broadfoot, P. (1991), 'The Impact of Current Changes in English Primary Schools on Teacher Professionalism', *AERA*, Chicago.

Osborn, M. and Pollard, A. (1991), 'Anxiety and Paradox: Teachers' Initial Responses to Change Under the National Curriculum', *Working Paper 4*, PACE Project, Bristol Polytechnic.

Richards, C. (1982), 'Curriculum Consistency', in Richards, C. (ed.), *New Directions in Primary Education*, Falmer Press, Lewes.

Silcock, P. (1990), 'Implementing the National Curriculum: Some Teachers' Dilemmas', *Education 3-13*, vol.18, no.3, pp4-11.

Simpson, E. (1988), *Review of Curriculum-led Staffing*, NFER Nelson, Windsor.

Simpson, E. (1990), 'The Stubborn Statistic', *Education*, no.21, April.

Smithers, A. and Zientek, P. (1991), *Gender, Primary Schools and the National Curriculum*, Birmingham, NAS/UWT.

Taylor, P. and Stanley, J. (1991), *Early Days: Primary School Teachers and the National Curriculum*, Primary Schools Research and Development Group, Birmingham.

Wicksteed, D. (1987), 'Curriculum Matters, Enough to Reduce It', *Education 3-13*, vol.15, no.2.

8

HAS POTENTIAL BUT MUST
TRY HARDER

DUNCAN GRAHAM

Duncan Graham was the first Chair and Chief Executive of the National Curriculum Council, appointed by Kenneth Baker in 1988. He resigned his post, in contentious circumstances, in 1991. He is a former Chief Education Officer for Suffolk and Chief Executive for Humberside. Since the resignation he has published a book on his experiences with the National Curriculum Council, A Lesson For Us All (1992). In this article, first published in the Observer on 6 September 1992, Duncan Graham argues that parents, not meddling Ministers, must take education forward.

Consensus is rare in the field of education. But it does exist about the national curriculum. How can England ever have managed without it? Debate is no longer about its existence, but about how to improve it.

Parents can be sure that, wherever they live, whatever the age and ability of their children, they will increasingly find a broad and balanced curriculum with clear objectives, a common grounding in the main subjects from ages five to sixteen and agreed standards for assessment – although the testing system is still experimental to say the least. The evidence is that standards are beginning to rise and inequalities are being ironed out. In spite of early fears, it has not become a 'straitjacket' for schools. As ever, schools are displaying a sturdy originality and variety in teaching approaches; the difference is that now these are sharply focused to the needs of individual pupils within better overall planning.

But should the universal joy be unconfined? Far from it! For what was created on the hoof has all the hallmarks of haste. Its machinery and language is cumbersome; it is overburdened with material – the subject working groups that drew up the content contained more zealots than cynics, always a dangerous ratio. The clash over whether children most need knowledge or skills is unresolved. Ideologues of the right seem to think that knowing about Mozart is more important than making music; those of the left claim that you can pick up grammar and numeracy by osmosis, as a kind of by-product of creative learning. A commonsense balance needs to be struck.

The national curriculum is too narrow if confined to traditional subjects. Efforts to reduce it to a core of basics need to be resisted, particularly when no one, least of all Ministers, seems quite sure what these are. Parents need to support schools, as industry does, in finding space for other things that matter. Before its politicisation, the National Curriculum Council gave sound advice on themes such as citizenship, health education, careers and environmental education, which most, but not all, schools have embraced.

The very success of the national curriculum poses the greatest threat to it. It is the number one target for hijacking by every pressure group, minority interest and nutcase in the land, together with all the legitimate interests, be they political, professional or parental.

Parents are now the most important of these. This is the central message of the White Paper, *Choice and Diversity*. In it, the Government declares that 'parents know better than educational theorists and administrators [what else would you expect!] and better even than our mostly excellent teachers.' Every parent reading this must take on board a front-line responsibility. It is they who must protect and improve their national curriculum. It would be fair to warn them that they had better come up with what the Government wants or they will soon share the fate of, and the contempt shown for, those poor educationists and administrators – not to mention the local education authorities and now apparently governors too – who will get it in the neck if their schools fail to conform. Parents should bear in mind too that, should they form any kinds of pressure groups, their views will be dismissed as those of 'professional parents'.

By now, if you are a parent, you will be beginning to feel a mite apprehensive. But it is your national curriculum and you will need to see it through the next critical phase. Here are a few tips about what you will be up against.

In the early days, Secretaries of State were careful not to meddle with syllabus content, or to tell teachers how to teach. Kenneth Baker, who can be regarded as the father of our curriculum, was well aware of the dangers of political interference. Inevitably though, the temptation proved too great and, by the time history and geography were introduced, personal prejudice had become apparent. It was not Parliament or the National Curriculum Council which decreed that history should stop in 1962, but a Secretary of State who apparently feared that the up-to-date stuff was too dangerous for pupils and teachers alike. Imagine studying Khrushchev and Kennedy without the demise of Communism.

History is only the most obvious subject where the 'correct', rather than the balanced, view can be slipped into the educational diet. When Kenneth Clarke began to tell primary teachers how to teach, preferring his own gut prejudice to the 'evidence, the warning signs were clear. With advice now coming from 'tame' advisory councils and an emasculated schools inspectorate, the risks are obvious.

Knowledge of facts is likely to matter much more than practical or problem-solving ability (is this what industry really needs?) and even now the moral crusaders are moving in with their own sets of values to peddle. Surely education should assist youngsters to identify their own positive values, rather than get them secondhand off a Victorian shelf? Unless Ministers and their friends can be persuaded to back off from the minutiae of the curriculum and allow change to follow from genuine and open debate, then we must fear the worst.

Watch out, too, for high ideals without resources. The national curriculum has been brought in at bargain basement prices. Money is not everything, but to spend markedly less than competitor nations; to cut back on equipment and capital investment . . . Have you ever heard of a firm introducing a new line without substantial development and servicing costs? You may wonder why teachers seem now to be even younger than policemen. Could it be that tyros cost locally managed schools a great deal less than experienced practitioners? We need new blood, not a wholeale haemorrhage of experience and maturity. If the national curriculum is as good as the Government claims, it needs investment.

There is every likelihood that the impact of the national curriculum could be lost in a welter of counter initiatives and distractions. Schools have lost count of the wheezes with which they have to cope. Parents consistently put small classes, good teaching and adequate equipment at the top of their shopping list. What they get is choice (which turns out to be for schools and not for them), bogus league tables, sponsored technology colleges for a privileged few (complete with Saatchi & Saatchi laboratories and Casio music rooms), four-yearly inspection by superannuated tenderers instead of HMI, and an upheaval of school organisation, opting out of what and to what end?

Parents may feel like opting out themselves by now. But a better idea would be to take every step towards creating a balanced partnership to support the new curriculum. Professionals do not know everything, but they do know something. Teachers need to feel part of the curriculum, rather than mere operatives. Industry and commerce need to be listened to – not just about 'the three Rs', but about their wish for good, broadly educated, responsible and motivated youngsters. Everyone needs to share in setting standards and in quality assurance. By destroying the old institutions without putting better in their place, the Government has created a black hole which, if left unfilled, will ensure that none of us know whether standards are rising or whether the national curriculum is working.

The National Curriculum is good news. For the first time we have a broadly acceptable indication of entitlement, of targets, of benchmarks and of standards. We all need to work hard on improving it in such a way that the education of each precious child is designed to realise its full potential and to maximise employment opportunities. We need to resource it adequately and to ignore the distractions. We need to protect it from those who seem to fear its success, and from those who recognise a good thing when they see it and want to make it *their* curriculum rather than the nation's.

PART III

9

BUY MY PIG IN A POKE

STUART MACLURE

Stuart Maclure was formerly editor of the Times Educational Supplement, *a post he held for many years. As an historian of education he is well-known for his* Educational Documents, England and Wales, *whose latest edition covers 1816-1986 (1986),* One Hundred Years of London Education, 1870-1970 *(1970) and* Education Re-Formed: A Guide to the Education Reform Act 1988 *(1988).*

In this article, the author argues that John Patten's White Paper, Choice and Diversity, *fails to answer the crucial funding questions that schools are now asking (*Times Educational Supplement, *4 September 1992).*

Is it my imagination or is this White Paper not unbelievably bad? Bad in the sense of poor quality – far below the standard you expect from a great department of state? Could you imagine David Eccles, Edward Boyle or Anthony Crosland – or for that matter, Margaret Thatcher or Keith Joseph – putting out such a slipshod and windy White Paper? And here is John Patten proudly boasting he wrote the first and worst chapter himself. *O tempora, O mores.*

Still, there it is: there has to be a White Paper (with a Bill to follow) because the Government expects a flood of applications for opting out, and for grant maintained (GM) status to become the norm. The document is meant to spell out what happens while this is taking place and after it is complete. The trouble is that it does so in such a way as to clarify very little for the governors of county and voluntary schools, whose decisions will determine how and when the changeover from a mainly local authority system to a mainly GM system takes place.

Let's start with the county schools, still the great majority of primary and secondary schools in England and Wales. The assumption is that they will go grant maintained in numbers. But will they? They will only opt out if they reckon they can get a better deal from the planned Funding Agency than their local education authority. But how will they decide? When will they be able to do the calculations – work out 'the nicely calculated less or more'?

All the Government says is that the future financial system will be based on the standard spending assessment (SSA), which is supposed to represent what needs to be spent to provide a standard level of education in each local authority area. A consultation document is to be issued in the autumn which will discuss the common funding formula (CFF) which the Funding Agency will use to distribute funds to individual schools.

The Government has an impossible circle to square. It wants to make it attractive for schools to opt out. But it wants even more to confine education spending within the standard spending assessment. Until now, a school (local authority or grant maintained) located in an area that spends more than its SSA assumes, benefits accordingly. (A few local authorities such as Kent and Birmingham spend less than their SSA, rather more spend more.)

If and when all the schools are under the Funding Agency, it will be much simpler for the Treasury to eliminate overspending. But it will result in a worse financial regime for a majority of schools.

Not only will schools contemplating opting out have to consider how they will fare when the standard spending assessment is rigidly enforced, they will also have to understand and evaluate the Funding Agency's CFF. Spokesmen can make soothing noises to their heart's content but no new formula can be devised within existing spending limits that does not produce winners and losers. Ministers will try to limit the range and provide safety nets, but whatever emerges will only be a first version of something they will go on tinkering with for crude political reasons, as they have rigged local authority grants in the past.

Meanwhile, the local authorities have already begun to work out 'nil retention' schemes of local management (where no cash is retained for central services). The Government will make others do the same. Full operating LMS schemes, coupled with the rest of the continuing uncertainty about GM funding, will give governors plenty to think about before they jump into John Patten's arms.

Nor will opting out be the only item on their agenda: secondary schools will also be deciding whether to specialise – become a magnet school, technology school or technology college. Admittedly, that means trying to make sense of chapter ten of the White Paper, a tall order. Anyone with a tame millionaire who might like to be a 'sponsor governor' will know exactly what to do. Others will be loth to buy the pig in this poke.

Voluntary school governors – meaning mainly, governors of Roman Catholic and Church of England aided schools – will have to do the same sums as county school governors, but will have the added inducement of knowing that if they opt out they cease to be liable for 15 per cent of any future capital spending.

The Churches remain suspicious of grant maintained status, which they see as divisive and potentially hostile to their own educational values. But it is not being cynical to guess that these scruples will be overcome and the Churches will accept the changes, thankful they are not worse.

The whole notion of the voluntary school is going to change radically if the paragraphs on the setting up of 'new grant-maintained schools' mean what they say. The sector will not just comprise existing Roman Catholic and Anglican schools and the handful of other schools, most linked to the other Christian denominations and Jewry. The door will be opened to any serious voluntary body that can raise the initial 15 per cent capital cost – see paragraph 4.11 – and make a persuasive case to the Funding Agency in any area where the proportion of pupils in GM schools has passed the 10 per cent mark. So Muslims will have their chance if they can teach the national curriculum without compromising their educational ideals. So will the Seventh Day Adventists, Plymouth Brethren and any other Evangelical Christian group that wants to invest large initial sums in education.

All this conjures up a heady vision of a suddenly expanding voluntary sector under the ample umbrella of the Funding Agency. Feed into this the hotchpotch of John Patten's magnet schools and life becomes even more unpredictable.

But you come down to earth with a bump when you read the sections on 'rationalisation' and the ritual incantations about elimination of surplus places. With one hand the Government promises more, and more diverse, schools; with the other, it promises to shut schools and take places out of service.

The idea of 'rationalisation' reintroduces the notion of an educational *system* – the concept of planning, of administrators sitting down and working out how many schools are needed where, and managing this famous market in education with a rod of iron. The Funding Agency – whatever Ministers may say – is going to have the job local authorities have done. It will decide which schools to suggest for closure. It will order existing schools to expand to take in more pupils. It will manipulate parental choices to make them fit the local schools. It will resist the creation of new GM schools where sufficient places already exist. Not only are we going to have an educational system; it looks as if we are going to have new local sub-systems too.

Or are we? These developments are all contingent on the Gadarene swine obliging the Prime Minister by making their mad rush for grant maintained status. This depends on the money; which depends on the funding formulae; which depends on the Treasury; which depends on the pound and the state of the economy. What a way, as they say, to run a railway.

10

DISSOLUTION IN ALL BUT NAME

MARGARET MADEN

After long experience as teacher and headteacher of comprehensive schools and a sixth form college, Margaret Maden is now Chief Education Officer for Warwickshire. She writes here on the future of local education authorities (from the Times Educational Supplement, *25 September 1992).*

At least with the dissolution of the monasteries there was a clear goal and the whole exercise was headed by an able administrator. In the case of the White Paper, however, the goals are diffuse and there doesn't appear to be a Thomas Cromwell to hand. Perhaps, though, the sub-text of *Choice and Diversity* has something in common with Cromwell's own belief that the monasteries were 'beyond reform' and that he first needed to persuade others of this if the Crown's purposes were to be served.

So that he could persuade Parliament of his views, a whistle-stop visitation (inspection) of monasteries was conducted by 'careerist secular clergy, imbued with the age-old dislike of seculars for regulars' (A.G. Dickens, *The English Reformation*).

Soon, self-appointed experts on monasticism could be found at every corner and in no time at all the climate of opinion had been changed. Parliament was regaled with lurid tales of monastic misdoings.

Not for us such crudity. Instead, the White Paper praises to the skies grant maintained schools and city technology colleges and the positive achievements of some 99 per cent of schools are largely ignored.

Other sins of omission are evident. The nexus of governors and headteachers working constructively with diocesan boards or with local authority members and officers is nowhere to be seen.

It is through this nexus, after all, that local management schemes have been successfully implemented through training programmes, new information technology systems and a good deal of mutual support and encouragement. This same local grouping has ensured that a helter-skelter pace of change has been made bearable and manageable.

Such realities of experience are put to one side and, as with Cromwell, there is a determined strategy running through the White Paper to change the climate of expectations and assumptions. This seems to be working in a surprisingly rapid way.

Last week I chaired a regional seminar organised for schools by the Government's Energy Efficiency Office. With a mixture of regret and bemused sense of loss, headteachers, bursars and governors prefaced their statements with such phrases as 'Now that we're losing local authorities'.

In that context, the assumed loss of local authorities meant that reliable and cost-effective expertise might not be available when energy audits need to be conducted or when new fuel tariffs have to be appraised. Longer-term capital investment needed for boiler replacement programmes and such like, would be subject to the vicissitudes of individual school bids and the random distribution of articulate governing bodies.

The discussion revealed a yawning gap between a rhetoric which insistently repeats the grant maintained message and the real concerns and priorities of people running schools.

But, unlike those monks and nuns of the sixteenth century, teachers, governors and parents have rights and duties in the secular state.

So much has been achieved in recent years and so much is now at stake. The Secretary of State will be helped if schools articulate *their* needs and priorities, both in the consultation period and during the passage of the Bill through both Houses.

That local nexus and, perhaps, the notion of praxis should be useful organising principles in any such analysis. For nexus, a linked group, represents at best the local authority and its partners; diocesan authorities, schools, community groups, employers and, embracing these, the local electorate, including parents.

Praxis, a model rooted in practice, provides a way of distilling and using practical experience so that a system which actually works can be designed and tested. If these two concepts are not seen or felt to be helpful and clarifying, then it must be back to the drawing board.

For, miles beyond party politics, the White Paper surely fails to provide a cost-effective or sturdy alternative to the present system, warts and all. If a better alternative can't be found, then perhaps we should return to Cromwell's monasteries as the sixteenth-century equivalent of local education authorities. The recently established Local Government Commission could conduct visitations up and down the land and report on the local administration of the education service.

Lurid revelations may emerge, although I suspect not. The strength of local authorities is often found in the quality of quite humdrum and modest support services and in the mastery of arcane, but rather important detail.

If the Commission was to be charged with implementing a new system, then it could still learn something from the dissolution process. Exemptions were initially granted to most Yorkshire monasteries to 'placate the northern malcontents', but more significantly to control the volume of religious persons seeking redeployment. For, having made his intentions clear, Cromwell at least offered a choice between dispensations (voluntary redundancy payments) and transfers to other religious houses.

Nuns, however, were discriminated against through a kind of Tudor 'double whammy'. They were not simply granted smaller pensions but were also barred from securing a second income through marriage.

Some of the bigger monasteries successfully resisted the earlier dissolution process, but ultimately to no avail. When government patience ran out, they were declared forfeit through being 'attainted of treason'. Dr Muffett, beware.

While historical analogies are notoriously suspect, I cannot resist drawing this one to a close by pointing out that Cromwell's masterful strategy failed. The purpose was to acquire, in perpetuity, vast amounts of money for the Crown so that Parliament's revenue-raising powers could be side-stepped. But the proceeds from the alienation of monastic lands were squandered and, in less than a century, yet another Cromwell rose to power and the King lost his head.

11

THE RIGHT TIGHTENS ITS GRIP ON EDUCATION

JUDITH JUDD AND NGAIO CREQUER

This article, by the educational correspondents of the Independent on Sunday, *was sub-titled 'John Patten is taking the "anti-trendy" revolution in our schools even farther than his predecessor' (from the* Independent on Sunday, *2 August 1992).*

Soon after he became Secretary of State for Education, Kenneth Clarke poked fun at the education world's love of acronyms – 'SEAC, what's that? The South-East Asia Consortium?'

It is, in fact, the School Examinations and Assessment Council, set up by statute in 1988 to advise on how children should be tested and examined.

Before he changed jobs nearly two years later, Mr Clarke's jovial mockery had become serious. The rout of the education establishment had begun – in came policy advisers who opposed 'trendy' education theories. A takeover of the education service by politicians, without parallel since the British government first became involved in schooling more than a century ago, was well underway.

Last week's education White Paper showed that John Patten, successor to Kenneth Clarke, wants to go even further. He wants a new national body to oversee schools that opt out, gradually taking education responsibilities away from local education authorities.

The new Funding Agency will respond to his direction and he will choose who sits on it. The National Curriculum Council (NCC) and SEAC, the exams council, will be merged to form one single bureaucracy.

The Secretary of State will have new powers to replace recalcitrant governors, intervene in disputes over admissions and reduce surplus places. Mr Clarke's appointment of Lord Griffiths as the head of SEAC was the clearest sign that education was to be taken out of the hands of educationists.

As head of Margaret Thatcher's Downing Street policy unit, Lord Griffiths had been the invisible overlord of education policy. A lay preacher, he is described as a man with a mission who had watched in dismay as the old establishment subverted the Government's reforms. He was also behind Margaret Thatcher's letter to Kenneth Baker in 1988 saying that the proposed national curriculum tests were too elaborate.

Appointments to SEAC and the NCC, which decides what children should be taught, are in the hands of the Secretary of State. The councils are being packed with members of the right-wing establishment. One analogy would be a Labour Government appointing Militant Tendency supporters to run the curriculum and tests.

Mr Patten recently confirmed that he intended to continue the work that Mr Clarke began by appointing John Marks, a member of a right-wing think-tank, to the NCC.

Dr Marks, an Open University tutor, who was made a member of SEAC two years ago, is the bogyman of the education world. He supports a return to selective schools, streaming by ability and traditional teaching methods.

His *Whose Schools? A Radical Manifesto*, written with Baroness Cox in 1986, contained many ideas that have since become Government policy. He wanted an external review of Her Majesty's Inspectorate, which he described as 'the dog that didn't bark'.

He joins a body that has already moved significantly to the right since it was established four years ago. So much so, according to critics, that it is in danger of failing to perform its statutory duty of giving the Secretary of State advice as he wants it and as it sees fit.

Peter Dines, former secretary of the SEAC, who retired last August, says the present regime 'is very close to being against the law. To fulfil its statutory functions it must be independent.'

The issue of whom the Government listens to came spectacularly to centre stage last month. Eric Bolton, who retired last year as the senior chief inspector of schools and is now professor of teacher education at London University's Institute of Education, told a conference of local education authorities that the Government was listening only to fashionable voices on the right, and that the influence of right-wing think-tanks on education appears stronger under John Major than it was under Mrs Thatcher.

It was not listening to heads, teachers, vice-chancellors, teacher trainers, exam boards or the HMI, he said. But it *was* listening to Dr Marks, the Centre for Policy Studies, and Dr Sheila Lawlor, the centre's deputy director.

'There is no crime in listening to your political friends,' Professor Bolton said. 'But a wise government listens more widely than that, and especially to those with no political axe to grind. It is not auspicious that the formal channels of advice about education to the Government appear either to be being muzzled (e.g., HMI), or packed with people likely to say whatever the Government wants to hear (the NCC and SEAC).'

It clearly touched a Government nerve. The following day, Baroness Blatch, education Minister of State, said she had to answer Professor Bolton's 'extraordinary' charges. 'The idea that we do not listen to people like HMIs, teachers, heads, or LEAs is simply blatant nonsense.'

Then she rounded on the educational professionals who, she said, had advised that the curriculum was best left to them, and had given us education without structure and education without grammar and spelling.

On the day Professor Bolton made his remarks, John Marenbon, a Cambridge don who is married to Dr Sheila Lawlor, was appointed to SEAC.

The influence of the Centre for Policy Studies is marked. Lord Griffiths chairs it, Dr Marks is secretary of its education study group, which also includes John McIntosh, headmaster of the opted-out London Oratory School and a member of the NCC.

The Educational Research Trust, whose aim is to promote research into education 'with particular reference to philosophical and religious principles', is also influential. Dr Marks is its director and advisers include Lord Griffiths, Mr McIntosh, and David Regan, professor of local government at Nottingham University and a member of the NCC.

The school curriculum and exams are being decided in the minutest detail from the centre by ministers and their political supporters. Decisions have been taken to:

Cut the proportion of coursework in the GCSE exam from 70 per cent to between 20 and 30 per cent.

Give all fourteen-year-olds tests on Shakespeare and grammar.

Include a study of the British Empire and more facts and dates in history.

Allocate 5 per cent of marks in the GCSE exam to spelling.

Do long division by a 'pencil and paper' method.

Order the Northern Examining Association to take references to *Coronation Street* and *Neighbours* out of its syllabus.

The break with the past is remarkable. Only ten years ago Britain was the only country in Europe that did not have a national curriculum and in which nothing was decided from the centre. The education establishment of teachers, lecturers and advisers may have had some control over the culture of education but its influence was limited and indirect. Power lay not with local education authorities or even heads, but with the individual classroom teachers.

The passing of the Education Reform Act in 1988 brought the teachers' freedom to an end. The Act gave the Secretary of State more than 400 new powers.

At first, it appeared that little would change. The first exam and curriculum councils drew their members from the dons, teachers and exam board officials who had staffed educational quangos in the past. The establishment was still in control.

With the arrival of the pugnacious Mr Clarke at the Department of Education in 1990, the position changed. Mr Clarke, fresh from duels with doctors at the Department of Health, turned on the teachers. He pushed through a series of changes to strengthen Whitehall's control of the curriculum and exams.

Mr Dines said: 'There has been a blatant shift to the right. Of course you need checks and balances to stop the professionals going barmy, but the Government wouldn't think of trying to run the oil business with civil servants and politicians.'

If the advisory bodies refused to do Mr Clarke's bidding, despite the injection of right-minded members, they were ignored. Decisions were taken hastily by small groups of Government supporters who aimed to replace the dogma of the left with that of the right.

While Lord Griffiths replaced Philip Halsey, a former civil servant of impeccable neutrality, at SEAC, David Pascall, a BP executive and also a former Downing Street adviser, took over from Duncan Graham, a former chief executive of Humberside County Council and county education officer in Suffolk, at the NCC. Both had educational credentials but the appointments were clearly political.

According to insiders, the arrival of Lord Griffiths transformed the atmosphere at Newcombe House in west London, SEAC's headquarters. 'To say that a climate of fear exists in Newcombe House would not be an exaggeration,' said one.

Mr Dines says: 'Mr Clark appointed him so that he would get the answers he wanted to hear. With Lord Griffiths as chairman the council is not in a position to make independent decisions.' The three main policy committees were abolished and details of the coursework changes were worked out at a private dinner attended by chosen members of the councils and hosted by Lord Griffiths.

Trusted members of the curriculum council travelled to London to meet ministers without the knowledge of its senior officials.

Lord Griffiths is a powerful chairman. One of his first decisions was to make it clear to the Department of Education and Science and HMI assessors that their presence was no longer required at meetings. He runs SEAC much as a company director would run his board. There are no votes.

According to the Government's critics, the Education Reform Act alone would not have led to ministerial interventions in the curriculum and testing if the Government had not placed its own supporters in powerful positions on the advisory bodies. But the extent of its patronage should not be exaggerated. Some independent-minded council members remain and argue their corner. According to one SEAC member, this has led to more arguments than ever before since August.

Mr Dines says: 'A lot of the important decisions, such as who gets the contracts for testing, are taken in between Council meetings. The Government has set up the Council as a watchdog, has first pulled out its teeth one by one, and then cut its head off. It is now a complete waste of money.' By the end of the year the two bodies will have spent more than £111m between them.

Who is deciding the content of the national curriculum tests that all children will have to take at seven, eleven and fourteen? Though independent groups are developing them, they are tightly controlled from the centre. One group working on English tests for fourteen-year-olds was told by an official that a question involving a passage from the *Sun* would have to go because 'ministers would not like anything involving pop stars.'

The *Sun* article reported a survey of children's fan letters, finding that more wrote to political figures and civil rights leaders they admired than to Jason Donovan and Kylie Minogue. For the test, pupils were asked to write a letter to someone they admired.

12

ITEMS FROM A CORRESPONDENCE BETWEEN FRED JARVIS AND THE PRIME MINISTER, JOHN MAJOR

During 1991 and 1992, Fred Jarvis conducted a correspondence with the Prime Minister on educational policy. During this period, Mr Jarvis received four communications from the Prime Minister's office, two of which were signed by John Major and two by members of his staff. Here the last two letters of this correspondence are reproduced: the first, from Jonathan Hill, the Prime Minister's political secretary, which summarises the Prime Minister's responses to questions asked by Mr Jarvis; and the second, comprising Mr Jarvis' response to this letter. No response had been received to Mr Jarvis' last letter (of 25 September 1992) at the time this book went to press.

10 Downing Street
London SW1A 2AA

9 September 1992

Dear Mr Jarvis,

I undertook to summarise the Prime Minister's responses to the various questions that you have posed at different stages of this lengthy correspondence. I apologise that you have had to wait longer for this than I envisaged when I last wrote.

The Prime Minister has set out in detail for you his ideals in education. These have been further outlined in his public speeches and reflected in the Government's recent White Paper, *Choice and Diversity*. I hope that you will feel able to accept those declarations of the Prime Minister's position and, as the Prime Minister has invited you in the correspondence, to work with the Government to improve standards in schools. It is noteworthy that many of the reforms in schools in the last few years which have been welcomed by parents and endorsed by the electorate have been opposed by the executives of the teaching unions. You will recall that the Prime Minister has asked you to use your influence to persuade them to support what is now proven to be a popular process of change.

In your letter of 27 June you make the claim that the Prime Minister has 'failed to provide answers to most of the questions' you have put to him since last July. With respect, I do not believe that to be the case: the Prime Minister has gone out of his way to reply to you on more than one occasion.

In your letter of 16 July 1991 you set out a number of questions:

1. You questioned whether there had been an insidious attack on literature and history in our schools.

I do not believe that there can be any dispute on this question. The National Curriculum Council has only recently recommended that the English order should be reformed partly in order to safeguard the teaching of our great literary heritage. And it is surely not without relevance that Mr Nigel de Gruchy, General Secretary of the NAS/UWT reacted to the Education Secretary's move to enshrine Shakespeare within national curriculum testing by saying it would be 'boring and irrelevant' for most children.

So far as history is concerned, the History Curriculum Association and the work of Freeman and McGovern have amply documented challenges to the traditional core of this crucial subject.

2. You challenged criticism of the sizeable bureaucracies in some Labour authorities, and invited the Prime Minister to explain his attitude to the role of LEA advisers and inspectors.

The Prime Minister believes each person is entitled to be judged on his or her merits. Many advisers and inspectors have done valuable work: but equally you will acknowledge the criticism that has been made, by HMI among others, of those in some authorities who have sought to impose on their schools highly contentious ideas, under the guise of 'good practice'. The reform of schools inspection and regular *independent* inspection of *all* schools was therefore one of the principles which the Prime Minister singled out as of particular importance in his letter of 17 February.

3. You claimed that it was a 'sweeping generalisation' to suggest that there were suspicions that standards are at risk in the way the GCSE has been implemented and asked for evidence. You implied that HMI did not share this view.

I believe you may now have seen the very important report by HMI into the conduct of the GCSE. HMI's more detailed work in 1992 followed preliminary studies in 1991 which had given them cause for concern. I simply do not think it is tenable to argue in the light of these independent findings by HMI that there is neither ground for suspicion that some standards are at risk, nor for the contention that some changes in procedures need to be considered. You will also be aware that HMI is not alone in having expressed doubts about quality control and the maintenance of standards in some aspects of GCSE.

4. You asked whether more money per pupil would be given to all schools.

The Government has in fact raised the level of spending per pupil significantly above those it inherited from Labour. But, as the Prime Minister explained to you at some length in his first letter, money per pupil is not so much the issue as how effectively resources are spent – one of the reasons the Government has advanced LMS.

5. You asked why the Government 'persisted with' CTCs.

Because they are popular with parents, because good science teaching needs strengthening, and because, as the Prime Minister has argued and the July White Paper underlines, *choice* and *diversity* are at the heart of Government policy.

6. You repeatedly questioned – even after the Prime Minister's speech to the Adam Smith Institute in June – whether the Government had any intention of helping children trapped in the worst performing schools.

I am sure you will accept that it is acting. The Prime Minister's words have now been reinforced by the White Paper, *Choice and Diversity*. I trust that the concept of Education Associations will win your support.

7. You asked where the Prime Minister stood on the re-organisation of schools to tackle surplus places.

I refer you to chapter four of *Choice and Diversity*.

8. You asked whether schools should not be seen as a 'whole community interest', rather than run in the interests of those 'whose children happen to be in them'.

The Government has done much to foster school–community links, including through the entrenchment of community governors. But, as the Prime Minister has repeatedly made clear, he believes that children have only one chance of a good education and their interests must be paramount.

9. You asked why the Government said nothing about pre-school education.

That is not the case. Pre-school provision has in fact expanded considerably, and action has been taken to help mothers. It is to be regretted that some local authorities are now harassing good and successful private nursery schools.

10. You ask whether the Prime Minister's statement that he has a high regard for the teaching profession can be believed.

It is not for me to say whether you or others will believe the Prime Minister's sincere and oft-repeated statements. But those statements lie on the record, as does the creation of an independent Review Body to assess teachers' pay.

Following the Prime Minister's detailed reply of 17 February you asked a whole series of supplementary questions. I note in passing that in that letter you condemned the widely respected work of Dr John Marks as that of 'a politically oriented pressure group'. The Government has a different view of Dr Marks' work, as his appointment to appropriate bodies has demonstrated. Your new, as opposed to repeated, questions were:

11. Why is the Government reducing the weight accorded to coursework in the GCSE?

The reasons for this were set out by the Education Secretary in announcing the Government's conclusions earlier this summer.

12. You asked a raft of questions which as the Prime Minister pointed out to you in his letter of 25 June were based on the 'false premise' that he was critical of comprehensive schools as such.

The Prime Minister has personally answered and rebutted those claims. And I hope that you will accept what he has written to you.

13. You asked whether the Government intended to restore the Eleven Plus exam.

It has no plans to do so, nor has anything the Prime Minister has said ever suggested it would.

You wrote a further letter on 8 May 1992, with yet more questions. In the main those repeated the allegation that the Government proposed the introduction of an Eleven Plus, and claimed there was an official policy aimed at 'selection'.

I refer you to chapter one of *Choice and Diversity* which sets out the Government's policy on specialisation and selection.

You wrote yet another letter on 24 June 1992. In the main this repeated many of your earlier contentions. But you added the claim that action to help deprived children in bad schools must mean a takeover by 'Whitehall'.

I refer you to chapter eleven of *Choice and Diversity* which corrects that distorted assertion, and sets out policy in detail.

You wrote yet another letter on 27 June 1992, in which, despite another detailed response from the Prime Minister to your enquiries, you still claimed he had not answered your questions. You repeated some and added more. The new questions were:

14. How will the Government combat damaging left-wing ideas in education?

Primarily, as the Prime Minister has argued by extending parental choice, so that parents can choose schools which provide the challenging and stretching learning they wish for their children. By intervening as appropriate, as the Education Secretary did on the matter of Shakespeare.

By discussion with the appropriate authorities, notably SEAC and NCC, who are now, for example, seeking a revision of the English order. By establishing a new Independent Inspectorate geared to measure primarily the objective product of education. And by the creation of a new School Curriculum and Assessment Authority which, as *Choice and Diversity* explains, will seek 'rigour, simplicity and clarity' in both the curriculum and the testing of it.

15. You question whether GM schools extend parental choice.

There is clearly a fundamental difference between your view of GM schools and that of the Prime Minister. There will be many more GM schools, wherever parents wish them. I refer you to chapter seven of *Choice and Diversity*.

I hope that, in view of the points set out in the letter, of the Prime Minister's personal replies to you, his widely welcomed speeches on education, and the further detailed statement of policy in the White Paper, *Choice and Diversity*, you will now accept that your points have been answered.

I cannot expect you to agree with the Prime Minister in every respect. But, whatever doubts you may have, I think there can be few subjects on which the British public have a better appreciation of his sincerity, clarity and determination.

Yours sincerely,

Jonathan Hill
Political Secretary

92 Hadley Road
NEW BARNET
Herts. EN5 5QR

25 September 1992

Dear Prime Minister,

I wish to thank you for your response to the various questions I have posed in the course of this lengthy correspondence, conveyed to me in Jonathan Hill's letter of 9 September. I much appreciate the fact that, at a time when you are beset by enormous pressures arising from the country's serious economic situation, you have been prepared to give consideration to the many issues I have raised.

You invite me to work with the Government to improve standards in schools. Given that much of my professional career was devoted to working and campaigning for greater investment in education, better educational provision and wider opportunities for all children, I would certainly be willing to work for those aspects of the Government's policies which I think might improve standards.

You also referred to the opposition by the executives of the teaching unions to many of your Government's measures in the last few years and asked that I should use my influence to persuade them to support what you say is 'now proven to be a popular process of change'.

At no time in this correspondence have I sought to speak on behalf of any teachers' union and would not seek to do so now. However, in my letter of 27 June I did comment on your Government's failure adequately to consult and work in co-operation with the teaching profession, the LEAs, the parents' and governors' organisations and suggested you ought to regard those bodies as your partners in the great task of providing high quality education for every child.

I further suggested that the prosecution of that task would benefit from a joint and dispassionate discussion of the needs, problems and achievements of our education system with those partners and other interests and I offered to play a part in the promotion of such discussion if you would agree to it.

Since you have made no response to my offer I repeat it now and with a greater sense of urgency. I hope you are as aware as I am of the continuing concern being expressed by many in the education service about various aspects of Government policy and Ministerial decisions. That concern will not have been lessened by the utterly inadequate time allowed by the Secretary of State for the submission of responses to the White Paper.

May I turn now to your response to the questions I have put to you, and particularly those put in my very first letter of 16 July 1991.

It is said by Mr Hill that you have gone out of your way to reply to me on more than one occasion, but I feel bound to point out that some of your statements in reply have themselves prompted further questions. In the four letters I have received from you – two signed by you and two sent on your behalf – answers have indeed been given to some of my questions and comments made on certain others. Nevertheless, and with great respect, I must also say that a number of important questions have not been answered or evidence provided, while some other questions have been recast in such a way that the actual question I asked has been evaded.

I will deal first with those questions which you have not answered or which have been recast and thereby evaded.

1. You will recall that I quoted your allegation that there was 'a mania that condemned children to fall short of their potential; that treated them as if they were identical or must be made so. A mania that undermined commonsense values in schools, rejected proven teaching methods, debased standards – or disposed of them altogether.'

I said that by implication you were accusing large numbers of teachers of responsibility for the situation you described and I asked on what evidence you based such a serious charge. You have not answered that question.

Since we have had Conservative governments for most of the period you were referring to, I also asked whether you apportioned any blame to your own Party for the alleged happenings. You have not answered that question.

2. I asked you to name the city education authorities who you said were 'employing more bureaucrats than teachers'. You have not named a single authority.

In November, Mr Peter Yorke replied on your behalf, sending me LACSAB figures which he claimed 'do indeed bear out the point that some city education authorities employ more bureaucrats than teachers'. The figures did no such thing. What they actually showed was that whoever advised you to make the statement I had questioned did not know the difference between a 'bureaucrat' and the many kinds of ancillary and support staff employed by all LEAS.

Mr Hill tried a different tack. He evaded the question I put and simply explained your attitude to the role of LEA advisers and inspectors.

3. Mr Hill says I had asked 'whether more money per pupil would be given to all schools'. I did not. I actually asked, in view of what you had said about the 'peaks of excellence' in the 'thriving private sector' setting an example for the whole education system, whether you were therefore prepared to see the schools attended by the large majority of the nation's children given as much money per pupil as the best private schools. You have not answered the question.

4. I said it was not surprising that places in the very limited number of City Technology Colleges were sought after, given the very generous funding of those institutions compared with local authority schools and asked if you favoured all schools being funded at the same level as the CTCs, and if not, why not. You have not answered those questions, or my question as to whether, in order to give 'deprived children in the bad schools in the worst boroughs' the extra help they ought to have, you would insist on the schools they attend being treated as favourably as the CTCs. I regret you did not consider that an issue worthy of comment.

While I fully recognise that dealing with the problems of such children and such schools is not only a question of money and resources, I believe it is morally and educationally indefensible that there should be such a wide gulf between the lavishly financed and equipped CTCs and the provision for the secondary schools in the inner city areas.

I asked why the Government had persisted with its CTC policy because it is clear that industry as a whole has not responded on anything like the scale originally envisaged. To say that parents now have a choice of sending their children to a CTC is simply not true for the vast majority of parents.

5. I asked why you had said nothing in your speeches about pre-school education. It is no answer for you to claim that pre-school education has expanded considerably. Most of that expansion has, of course, been undertaken by the Labour local authorities you are normally so anxious to criticise. There are whole areas of the country where pre-school provision is very limited indeed, and as a whole this country is well behind the leading members of the EC in this field.

I repeat my question: since you have had so much to say about 'real choice' for parents, why do you remain silent about the pre-school education which so many parents would like to choose for their children?

I find your silence on this subject very disappointing and that of the White Paper, which purports to detail 'the final stages' of the 'great transformation in education', simply astounding. Have you no ambition to fulfil the promise held out by your predecessor nearly twenty years ago, and to take a step which many regard as far more important than a lot of the developments on which the Government is choosing to spend its energies and our taxes?

It is regrettable that while you propose to spend money to erect a new and complex bureaucracy you do not envisage providing more money for pre-school education.

You say it is to be regretted that some local authorities are now 'harassing good and successful private nursery schools'. I would like to know what evidence you have for that charge, given your failure to provide evidence to substantiate your charge about the employment of bureaucrats.

6. I did not ask whether your statement of your high regard for the teaching profession could be believed, but whether you seriously thought teachers would believe you after the treatment they had received at the hands of the Conservative Government and your refusal to contemplate the establishment of a General Teaching Council. In February I again asked about the GTC but you have not answered.

Rather than refer to the Pay Review Body, on which opinion within the profession was divided, do you not think it would be more helpful to your relations with teachers if you had shown willingness to consider a proposal on which the whole profession is united, and which has the support of the Select Committee and many of your own backbenchers?

7. You will be aware that I asked what evidence you could produce to substantiate a number of sweeping allegations you had made in your two speeches. One of those related to what you had called the 'insidious attacks on literature and history in our schools'.

I am not sure which reply is the more pathetic and lacking in intellectual integrity – that given on your behalf in November by Mr Yorke or your present response, conveyed by Mr Hill.

Mr Yorke offered as 'evidence' ludicrous statements about Jean-Jacques Rousseau and John Dewey, alleged repudiation by humanities departments in American universities of 'the canons of western civilisation in favour of multiculturalism', the experience of 'one school teacher employed by one of our LEAs', and the 'politically correct' movement 'currently raging through the American universities'.

You now say you do not believe 'there can be any dispute on this question' and offer as your 'evidence' the recent recommendation of the National Curriculum Council for the partial reform of the English order and a comment by Mr Nigel de Gruchy about the teaching of Shakespeare.

I will not dwell on the strong criticisms which have been made of the NCC's decision, not least those made by Professor Brian Cox, a person appointed by the Conservative Government to chair the NCC's English working party, but I doubt very much whether most members of the NCC who supported the recommendation did so because they believed 'insidious' attacks on literature were taking place in our schools. Equally, I am surprised you should regard one remark by Mr Nigel de Gruchy, made more than a year after you made your allegation, as evidence of what is actually happening in our schools.

As to your evidence of insidious attacks on history, are you seriously suggesting that the work of two individual teachers who lost their jobs in one school, and the activities of a tiny association which is made up of the same two people plus Robert Skidelsky, who happened to have a pupil at the same school, plus a few other people, 'amply documents challenges to the traditional core of this crucial subject'? Any university student who offered that kind of answer to an examiner would rightly deserve to be penalised for sheer lack of intellectual rigour.

Since you have referred elsewhere in your letter to evidence collected by HM Inspectorate, I invite you to say what evidence, if any, the Inspectorate has collected in relation to the 'insidious attacks on literature and history' of which you have spoken. I am sure you would agree that if your allegations were true that ought to have been a matter for investigation by HMI, so I hope you will agree to furnish any evidence the Inspectorate has produced. I also invite you to say whether the Historical Association, a far more representative body that the 'History Curriculum Association', shares your view about the teaching of history.

8. There is a similar lack of intellectual rigour, or in this case integrity, in your response to what I had to say about the whole community's interest in the provision of education and the work of schools. I did not ask 'whether schools should not be seen as a "whole community interest" rather than run in the interest of those "whose children happen to be in them" ' and I would not for one moment disagree with your belief that children have only one chance of a good education and that their interests should be paramount. Indeed, that is why I have been so critical of aspects of your Government's policies over the years and have regretted the failure of the nation under successive governments to invest on the scale necessary to provide high quality education for every child.

The point I was raising, and which you have not dealt with, is that the Government's policy in respect of opted-out schools seems to be based on the assumption that individual schools are owned and have been paid for by the parents whose children happen to be in them at a particular point in time and, therefore, it is those parents alone who should decide whether the school should opt out of the local education community. Your policy does not even allow the parents of all concerned about the future of the school, to have a voice, and equally it does not allow a later generation of parents to vote for the school to return to the local education community should they wish it to do so.

Since you talk so much about 'accountability', by what means is a grant maintained school made accountable to the taxpayers and poll-taxpayers of the whole community in which it is situated who, along with the parents directly involved in its affairs, have a strong interest in the quality of the education the school is providing and which they are helping to pay for?

I regret your Government's hostility to local democracy is so strong as to make it seek virtually to destroy the responsibility of local communities, through their democratically elected local authorities, for educational provision in a manner which takes into account the needs for all the children in a given community.

Local authorities of all political complexions, including many run by your own Party, are justifiably proud of their schools and colleges and the vital part education plays in their affairs. They are right to fear the effects of your intention to impose what *The Times* has described as the 'nationalisation' of the country's schools, accompanied by a bureaucratic structure which will be accountable to nobody but the Secretary of State.

9. You spoke last year of the grant maintained schools as the institutions to 'break the mould of political extremism and bureaucratic inefficiency'. I pointed out that the majority of the relatively small number of schools which had opted out had been in Conservative LEAs and I asked whether you were accusing those authorities of political extremism and bureaucratic inefficiency. You have not answered the question.

You have, however, answered my question about your position on the reorganisation of schools to save money being spent on surplus places, by referring to chapter four of the White Paper. I am glad that the White Paper recognises that LEAs should make sensible, comprehensive proposals concerning all their schools and I agree that is essential if the most rational use of resources is to be achieved. It is precisely because some schools have, in the recent past, sought to prevent their LEA carrying out that responsibility by 'opting out' and have met with Government approval that I shall wait with great interest to see how the present Secretary deals with the applications of such schools for grant maintained status.

10. You suggest that the 'raft of questions' about your attitude to comprehensive education in my letter of 27 February was based on the 'false premise' that you were critical of comprehensive schools as such, and you say you have personally answered and rebutted my claims.

In fact, the questions I put, and which you have not answered, were not based on any false premise. They were based on, and entirely relevant to, your own statement that you had been 'drawn to the view that the problem of low standards stems in large part from the nature of the comprehensive system which the Labour Party ushered in in the 1960s'.

I know I am not alone in finding it difficult to understand how you can be so critical of the 'comprehensive system', yet claim that you are not critical of 'comprehensive schools as such'. What comprises the comprehensive 'system' other than the totality of the comprehensive schools within it?

What is incontestable, however, is that whereas in July 1991 you did not even mention comprehensive education, by last February you had come to the conclusion that the system which is operated by virtually all LEAs – Labour, Conservative and Liberal Democrat alike – is largely responsible for the problem of low standards. Whatever it was you were actually blaming, a system or the schools which comprise it, I think the public is still entitled to know how you reconcile your talk of low standards with what you said in July 1991 about the 'success story' represented by the sharp rise in the proportion of our young people benefitting from higher education.

More recently still, your own White Paper proclaimed the achievements of the young people of Wales. It said: 'the proportion of young people leaving school with recognised qualifications has increased significantly, as has the number of pupils entering full-time further and higher education.' Yet those young people have come almost entirely from comprehensive schools. Do you suggest those schools are responsible for 'low standards'?

Since you had spoken of your determination to 'reverse the failings of the comprehensive system' I asked how you intended to do that and, in particular, whether it was your intention to reintroduce selection at Eleven Plus, or allow it to re-emerge via the back door.

Having received no answer, and having listened to your 'Election Call' broadcast in which you failed to state where you stood on the issue, I then asked further questions in my letter of 8 May. If you re-read that letter you will find I did not, as you claim, repeat 'the allegation that the Government proposed the introduction of an Eleven Plus' or claim that there was 'an official policy aimed at selection'.

I did, of course, quote *The Times'* view that what was happening under your Government's policies was a return to the system prior to 1965, and I did state that selection is being reintroduced as a result of the 'opting out' process (something I do not think you can deny), but all my questions were directed at trying to find out where you stood on the issue of selection.

I am, therefore, grateful for your statement now that the Government has no plans to restore the Eleven Plus examination, though the statement in the White Paper to the effect that the Government will neither encourage or discourage applications from non-selective schools to become selective suggests that you are prepared, as Kenneth Clarke clearly implied before the election, to contemplate the re-emergence of selection via the back door. You will also concede, I think, that the Government has departed from the undertaking given by Kenneth Baker that opted-out schools would not be allowed to change their character for at least five years after opting out.

You will appreciate that my questions about selection followed from my attempt to establish how you intended to reverse the 'failings' of the comprehensive system. One way of doing that, of course, would be to get rid of comprehensive education altogether and bring back the kind of selective system we had before which failed vast numbers of our young people. That would, however, involve the Government taking a view on the key issue of selection, which you appear unwilling to do. That being the case, most secondary schools are likely to remain comprehensive, so it is not unreasonable to ask again – what do you intend to do to remedy what you have called their 'failings'?

11. You say I was wrong to assert that the action you contemplate to help deprived children in bad schools meant a 'takeover' by Whitehall. Anybody who reads the chapter of the White Paper to

which you referred me can have little doubt that the Secretary of State's intention is, indeed, to take over, via the Education Association which he appoints and which is accountable to him alone, a failing school if, in his judgement, the action of the governing body or the LEA is deemed inadequate.

This is yet one more example of the great increase in the powers of the Secretary of State which the White Paper envisages. I am, therefore, even more anxious to know how you reconcile that further accretion of power, and the hundreds of new powers secured under the Baker Act, with the criticism you made in your Adam Smith Institute speech of the state arrogating to itself more and more powers and your attempt to rebut accusations that your Government is taking power from others in order to exercise it in Whitehall. Perhaps you would care to deal with that point?

I apologise for the length of this letter, occasioned by the need to deal with the many points you have raised, but there are certain other issues on which I must comment.

The first concerns the GCSE. I did say it was my recollection that HM Inspectors had claimed the GCSE was a success and that the previous Secretaries of State had also claimed it was a great success. I therefore asked what evidence had caused you to repudiate the views of your ministerial colleagues.

Now we have had the new Secretary of State causing immense concern among pupils, parents and teachers by his extraordinary behaviour in dealing with an unpublished report of the Inspectors – behaviour which was in marked contrast to that of the Minister for Schools, Mr Forth – one is tempted to ask which colleague you prefer to believe.

However, I recognise that there are issues to be addressed in the light of the Inspectors' reports. What ought to concern you is the standpoint from which they should be addressed and with what object in view. Notwithstanding the fact that the GCSE was introduced and has been overseen by a Council established by a Conservative Government, you will be aware that there are those close to you who want to get rid of the GCSE and return to the previous examination arrangements and are seeking to use the Inspectors' reports to that end.

It emerges from the Inspectors' reports, however, that many of the criticisms they make are neither new nor easy to resolve – an important point to which Mr Patten chose not to draw attention when, contrary to all normal practice, he released selected parts of the latest report in advance of publication of the full report, and within days of the statement of Mr Forth praising this year's GCSE results. He chose also not to refer to the problems which arose as a result of his predecessors' insistence, at a late stage, that the examining boards should take account of spelling, punctuation and grammar.

It would appear, also, that many of the points made by the Inspectorate on the working of the GCSE bear a striking similarity to the report of the Commons' Select Committee when it complained in 1977 of the uneven quality in the awarding of GCE 'O' level grades. Moreover, the former Head of the Inspectorate has declared that comparability has always been a problem, as has the variability of examination papers, and the Inspectorate were telling the Secretary of State what they have told him in the past.

Since Mr Patten must have been aware of the previous criticisms, and that steps had already been taken to deal with the criticisms made in the previous HMI report, his behaviour seems irresponsible as well as extraordinary.

I am sure you would do a great deal to reassure pupils, parents and the teaching profession if you were to make clear that while the Government expects the examination boards to deal with the issues raised by the Inspectors' reports it does not intend to change the basic character, purpose and procedures of the GCSE and has no intention of reverting to the previous examination arrangements.

On GM schools, there is indeed a fundamental difference between us but I believe events will demonstrate, as they have already begun to indicate, that far from enlarging parental choice, for many there will be a diminution of choice.

From what you say about the way you intend to 'root out left-wing ideas in education', I get the impression that you seek to dismiss any thinking not in accord with the Government's own narrow and ideologically charged view, as 'left-wing'. That is the kind of sweeping generalisation which I have cited, and challenged, from your two speeches and which you have signally failed to justify in the course of our correspondence.

I am bound to say that while I respect your sincerity, I do not believe you can afford to alienate large sections of the education community in the way that you and your Secretary of State are doing. One further example of what I have in mind is recent appointments to the official bodies advising on aspects of education policy.

It has been widely observed in the press that you are increasingly appointing right-wing ideologues to those bodies and your reference to Dr Marks does not disprove the point. Such action is likely to undermine the confidence and respect which those bodies need from the education community.

I am clearly not alone in taking that view. The statements recently made by such widely respected educationists as Professor Brian Cox, Professor Paul Black and Mr Duncan Graham, for example, reflect the same concern. They were themselves appointed by your Government to very important posts and have spoken from direct experience of the developments they have criticised.

Their concern and mine, and that of many others, was most eloquently expressed by the former Head of the Inspectorate, Professor Eric Bolton when he said at this year's CLEA conference: 'the Government shows little sign of being a listening government. When it does listen it does so so selectively that most of those in the education service fear what they have to say falls on deaf ears. There is no crime in listening to your political friends. But a wise government listens more widely than that, and especially to those with no political axe to grind. It is not auspicious that the formal channels of advice about education to the Government appear to be either muzzled (e.g., HMI) or packed with people likely to say whatever the Government wants to hear (the NCC and SEAC) . . . It [the Government] listens so selectively and has so firmly closed the windows that it does not seem to hear, or see, the education scene as most people out in the world experience it.'

You may not wish to heed my words but I think you would be very unwise to ignore those of people like Professor Bolton.

While you might prefer to continue to avoid answering some of the questions I have put to you, I hope you will consider the suggestion I repeated at the beginning of this letter and enter into serious discussions with the representatives of parents, teachers, governors, the local education authorities and others concerned with education to consider the real needs, problems, tasks and achievements of the education service. If I can assist that process in any way I shall be very pleased to do so.

Yours sincerely,

Fred Jarvis

13

CONSERVATIVE PARTY CONFERENCE, 1992

Extracts from speeches by the Rt Hon. John Major MP, the Prime Minister and Leader of the Conservative Party, and by the Rt Hon. John Patten MP, Secretary of State for Education, to the 109th Conservative Party Conference at Brighton early in October 1992.

EXTRACT FROM JOHN MAJOR'S SPEECH

When it comes to education, my critics say I'm 'old-fashioned'. Old-fashioned? Reading and writing? Spelling and sums? Great literature – and standard English grammar? Old-fashioned? Tests and tables? British history? A proper grounding in science? Discipline and self-respect? Old-fashioned?

Well, if I'm old-fashioned, so be it. So are the vast majority of Britain's parents. And I have this message for the progressives who are trying to change the exams. English examinations should be about literature, not soap opera. And I promise you this. There'll be no GCSEs in 'Eldorado'.

I also want reform of teacher training. Let us return to basic subject teaching, not courses in the theory of education.

Primary teachers should learn how to teach children to read, not waste their time on the politics of gender, race and class.

I don't know if you feel as I do, but I think it is intolerable that children should spend years in school and then leave unable to read or add up. It is a terrible waste of young lives.

We want high standards, sound learning, diversity and choice in all our schools. But, in some – particularly in those inner cities – Isaac Newton would not have learned to count, and William Wordsworth would never have learned to write.

We cannot abandon the children in schools like these. And we will not. So if local authorities cannot do the job, then we will give the job to others.

In the place of the local authority which has failed, new Education Associations will be set up to run and revive these schools. Governments have always shied away from it. But I am not prepared to do so any longer.

Yes, it will mean another colossal row with the educational establishment. I look forward to that. It's a row worth having. A row where we will have the vast majority of parents – and the vast majority of good, committed teachers – squarely on our side. They believe what we believe – that children must come first.

EXTRACT FROM JOHN PATTEN'S SPEECH

First, let me introduce my ministerial team: my right-hand woman and marvellous deputy Emily Blatch. Next to her, Eric Forth, our Schools Minister, scourge of sloppy standards and Labour LEAs. Then, Nigel Forman, who as a former university lecturer, has turned gamekeeper as our Minister for Higher Education. Our ironclad Whips, Andrew Mackay, and Giles Goschen from the Lords. Next to them, our much valued PPSs, Matthew Carrington and David Evennett. And finally, James Pawsey, the ever forceful and watchful Chairman of our Education Committee in the House of Commons.

That is the team. It's a completely new team; housed in a new building; and with a new name: no longer the Department of Education, now the Department for Education.

A new team – serving a Prime Minister who has put Education at the very top of his agenda – helping to take forward the great education reforms of the 1980s: some of the most radical and exciting political changes – not just of the last thirteen years – but of the whole of the postwar period.

We will soon be facing a new Labour team in the House of Commons. I have to say, they've been pretty slow off the mark. We've heard very little from them. They're obviously a modest lot. But then, they've got a lot to be modest about.

They've certainly been handed a poisoned chalice by their new leader – a man who during his leadership campaign didn't exactly put education at the top of his agenda. In fact, it never made his agenda.

Even the *Times Educational Supplement* last week acknowledged that '. . . Mr Smith has never majored in education.'

Never majored in it? He never mentions it. There is only one party leader who majors in education. John Major.

Ladies and gentlemen, while Labour's agenda for education is empty and confused, ours is full and clear.

We believe in greater choice and diversity, in ensuring that every child is equipped for adult life.

We want the best system of education in order to benefit all – not just a few. To achieve the best, we must raise standards.

There are no short cuts to a good education.

Children have to learn the basics.

That's what parents want.

That's what children need.

And that's why we believe in the three 'Rs'.

Ladies and gentlemen.

We have many excellent teachers in this country. They are dedicated professionals. I pay tribute to them.

They've had a busy time of late. In our drive to raise standards, we have given them a lot to do. I recognise that. And I applaud them for the way they have risen to the challenge.

Teaching is not an easy job. But all the more reason for teachers to have the full support and co-operation of parents: to know that the pupils in their class will arrive at school on time, properly turned out, ready for a day's schooling and with a clear understanding of what is right and what is wrong.

Under the Parent's Charter, we have opened up the education world as never before, giving parents a host of new rights. But with those rights come responsibilities.

Sometimes that may mean turning off the TV. Did you know that a majority of five-to-seven-year-olds spend more time in front of the television than they do in front of the blackboard?

That cannot be right.

Parents must give a lead.

But all too often, the problems in education lie – not with parents, not with teachers – but with the 1960s theorists, with the trendy left, and with the teachers' union bosses.

Some seem to think that children shouldn't be taught the alphabet. Others think children shouldn't be tested. One union leader even said, 'spelling surely can't be important.'

Mr chairman, I recently announced that all fourteen-year-olds are to be tested on a set Shakespeare play.

Do you know what one union leader said? You 'try and teach Shakespeare to some of our budding football hooligans' and that my proposal was 'fine for grammar school kids, but . . . would be boring and irrelevant for a good half of pupils'.

How patronising!

How defeatist!

Our children deserve better than that.

And with this Conservative Government they'll get better than that.

But I am afraid that the interests of children are not served either by some of the examination boards. One recently defended the use of a hamburger advertisement in a public exam by claiming that it provided just as important 'food for thought' for children as our great literary heritage.

They'd give us Chaucer with chips.

Milton with mayonnaise.

Mr Chairman, I want William Shakespeare in our classrooms, not Ronald McDonald.

Her Majesty's Inspectors have recently provided me with some food for thought about the exam boards themselves.

The Inspectors' independent report on GCSEs may not have been very palatable, but we will never compromise on standards. In just thirty weeks time, another group of children will sit down to take their GCSEs. I am determined to see that public confidence in those examinations is maintained and that teachers and, above all, pupils, are not let down.

Of course, it is hard for parents to have much confidence in the exam boards when some of them include television programmes such as 'Neighbours' and even ''Allo, 'Allo' in their English syllabuses.

Well, I have a message for those exam boards. 'Listen very carefully. I will say this only once. "Get your act together!" ' The litany of educational let-down has gone on long enough.

Ladies and gentlemen.

We have already gone a long way towards achieving our goals in education.

The recent White Paper provides the keystone to our reforms.

I do not have to remind this conference, and especially our excellent councillors, that our commitment to the grant maintained revolution was a central plank of the manifesto on which we fought the recent election. It will remain at the heart of our policy on education.

I want to see all schools going grant maintained.

We will, as a priority, sweep away the barriers erected against schools who want to opt out of local authority control.

Grant maintained schools know how it feels to have decisions taken – not by Government, not by local education authorities – but by those who care most about the school and are closest to it: the parents, the teachers and the members of the local community.

They decide what the priorities are. They take the decisions. And they take them much quicker than a bureaucracy ever can.

That's local accountability at its best.

And it's education at its most effective.

Self-governing schools have a vested interest in getting rid of waste and in getting maximum value for money for their pupils.

It is now common practice for GM schools to appoint a bursar. At one GM school, King Edward VI, Louth in Lincolnshire, the bursar saved the school his own salary in the first year through re-negotiating contracts and getting the best purchasing deals. The school not only got back the bursar's salary, but also gained the extra teaching time of the Head and his senior staff.

Yet, shamefully, some local authorities squander public money on discouraging parents from balloting.

This abuse of public funds has got to stop. And it will stop.

And not before time, you might say if you come from Labour-controlled Lambeth. Or Birmingham for that matter. What a pig's ear they've made of trying to run education in England's second city.

Yes, Birmingham, the socialist authority that wastes millions on maintaining half-empty school buildings.

Socialist Birmingham, the authority that hijacks money earmarked by the Government for education, to spend on 'other' priorities.

Birmingham, the socialist authority that fights GM applications by parents with some of the most malicious and vindictive tactics.

And, not surprisingly, Birmingham, the socialist authority that turns in some of the worst exam results in the whole country.

Somebody ought to tell the Labour group in Birmingham that LEA doesn't stand for 'Leave Education Alone'.

Ladies and gentlemen.

Just as we need to ensure that our children are well taught, so we need to be certain that our teachers are practically trained – not with the discredited theories of the 1960s, but as much as possible at the chalkface, in the classroom.

More time needs to be spent providing teachers-to-be with experience of what actually happens in the classroom.

Some schools are coming to me and asking if they can take on the responsibility for training teachers.

We have already announced a move towards more training within schools.

That is just a first step. We need to go further and we will go further.

But I also want to extend the routes into teaching: to give greater opportunities to those who have already raised a family and have something to offer to our young school children.

These are all vital measures and form an intrinsic part of our philosophy. How do they compare with our opponents' educational philosophy?

We don't know, because they don't seem to have one. As far as I can discern any guiding principle, it appears to be: first, vehemently oppose whatever the Government proposes, however sensible the policy; then, when the policy is clearly working and is proving popular, announce that you see some merit in it after all.

Look at their record.

We proposed a national curriculum; they opposed it, then made it Labour policy.

We proposed local management of schools; they opposed it, then made it Labour policy.

Perhaps one day Labour will have an original idea of its own. But somehow I doubt it.

Last week in Blackpool, the Labour Party nailed its anti-choice colours firmly to the mast. The conference approved a motion, backed by the Party leadership, to fight applications for self-governing schools 'vigorously' and 'at every opportunity'.

The motion was proposed by the Socialist Education Association.

Just when we thought that socialism had become the vice that dare not speak its name, so once again it has raised its ugly head in Labour Party circles.

Oh yes, it's back to the past for Labour.

No mention in their Party Conference motion about higher standards in education.

No recognition of the importance of basics.

No account taken of the wishes of parents.

What's Labour afraid of?

'I'll tell you what – the voice and the choice of parents, that's what

Labour's afraid of.

And where do the Liberals stand, those self-proclaimed champions of the individual and of community involvement?

I'll tell you where they stand on self-governing, grant maintained schools. Shoulder to shoulder with the socialists. That's where you'll find Captain Ashdown and his friends.

Ladies and gentlemen.

We have many excellent colleges and universities in this country. We have some of the best lecturers and researchers in the world.

We have two key aims: to raise standards in higher education and to make sure more people get a chance to go on to further and higher education.

Look at our record.

More eighteen-year-olds than ever before are now going on to higher education. In our manifesto, we stated that the number going into full-time higher education would rise to one in three by the year 2000. We are set not only to reach that figure, but to surpass it.

That will be a remarkable achievement for this Conservative Government, one that augurs well for the future prosperity of this country.

Most students who go on to college or to university do so because they want a good education and a qualification that they can use to get on in life.

It's only a few who get involved through the National Union of Students in supporting dubious causes of no interest to other students.

In a free country, that is their privilege.

But why should the taxpayer have to pay for it?

It has always been our aim as a Party to preserve and extend personal liberty and freedom of choice.

I will therefore bring forward proposals to establish the voluntary principle as the basis for student union membership.

We have abolished the closed shop everywhere else. There is no reason why it should linger on in our colleges and universities.

The NUS closed shop must go.

And it will go. Soon.

To me, education is everything. Our very civilisation, our way of life, our capacity to compete, our ability to live as responsible, caring individuals are all built on the rock of education.

I tell you this.

We are the Party of education.

It's our agenda.

We've given the lead. Our opponents have nothing new to say. Nothing new to offer.

We are the ones with vision for our children. Look at what we have already achieved.

the national curriculum;

regular testing for all our children;

more information, publicly available through the Parent's Charter;

more freedom for our schools;

greater choice and more diversity;

better – and more frequent – inspection of all our schools; and

more power for parents and governors.

That's how we are creating a more open, a more responsive and a more demanding system of education.

Standards are rising.

More children are staying on at school.

More eighteen-year-olds are going on to university than ever before.

To compete in the twenty-first century, we will need the best technicians and engineers, the best designers and managers, the best, most highly motivated workforce.

Such talent can only be produced by a first-class education system.

Who will sustain our cherished NHS without bright young people to generate the resources to pay for it?

What use is the single market if we don't have the talent and initiative of a well educated workforce to exploit that market?

I want the years ahead to be golden years for our young people, the harvest years when we as a nation reap the benefits of the fundamental changes we have made and are making.

And just as before, when the world turned to Britain – for our legal system, for our inventive genius, for our parliamentary democracy, so I want the world in the years ahead, to turn to Britain in admiration of our education system.

I will not be satisfied until our young people are the best educated in the world. This demands an education system that meets the aspirations of parents.

It demands a system that gives parents the opportunity to choose the right school for their child.

It demands, not uniformity, but diversity and choice.

It demands the very highest standards of teaching.

And it demands a crusade to bring out the best in Britain's youth.

Those are our demands.

We have to meet them.

And we will.

Appendix 1
STATE KNOWS BEST

*The publication of John Patten's White Paper at the end of July 1992
was greeted by the following leader in* The Times *(29 July 1992).*

The Government is dismayed at Britain's poor education record and
has responded as governments always respond. It has blamed
everybody but itself, and decided to nationalise the schools.

John Patten's White Paper entrenches the already centralised
curriculum. But that is not its prime purpose. This is eventually to
remove schools from local authority control and bring them under
what is to be a powerful new central funding agency. The White Paper
envisages that all 25,000 secondary and primary schools in England
and Wales may one day come under this agency, as local education
authorities wither.

This is one of the most dramatic extensions of Whitehall power seen
since the war. This is no free market in education. The White Paper is
filled with new powers to be conferred on the funding agency and
other quangos, whose officials will fill office blocks the length and
breadth of the land. Schools funded locally are to come within the
scope of Whitehall's new schools planners as soon as 10 per cent of
places locally are 'opted out' of local council control. Local schools
will be taken over by the state when the proportion rises to 75 per cent.
This is a devastating vote of no confidence in local democracy.

The need for centralisation is a mystery. The Government's own
local management of schools (LMS) initiative was already cutting
bureaucracy and giving schools the autonomy that most parents and
teachers want in order to save money and raise standards. This could
be extended. But the bonds that tie schools to their communities
through local democracy – bonds nowhere mentioned in the White
Paper – are long-standing and the source of great pride. It is
extraordinary that a Conservative Government should have such

contempt for them and such faith in the rectitude of Whitehall planning. Nationalisation will make schools more, not less, uniform, as it has done prisons and hospitals. The powers Mr Patten is taking to himself are gargantuan.

The Government has not thought through its search for 'diversity, parental choice, specialism and standards' in the resulting school system. The pattern most likely to emerge is roughly comparable to that obtaining under the 1944 Act, prior to the 1965 comprehensive reorganisation. This means finding some way of deciding a child's educational future at about the age of eleven – long regarded as too early. After 1944 an attempt was made to make the 'choice' of school at eleven as fair as possible, by testing aptitude objectively and allocating children to different types of school, each enjoying 'parity of esteem'. Parents and children not selected for their chosen (usually grammar) school were thus supposed not to feel rejected. Never was elitist supposition so false.

Popular schools are those that get good academic results. They get good results by being academically selective, not by admitting any children whose parents ask. This cannot be dodged by wallowing in Mr Patten's ceaseless platitudes. He would have done better to recall the ambitions of the 1944 Act, explain his belief in selection, and explain his plans for the 'reject' sector. This sector may be smaller than before comprehensive reorganisation, but that will make the deprivation the greater, for parents, teachers and pupils alike. Mr Patten is not even offering those rejected the advantage of a 'loaded voucher', so that what are already being known as sink schools can at least have extra money. He is merely pretending that every school will have 'equality of esteem' and that nobody should feel rejected. Bad schools will experience instant nationalisation under an 'education association' appointed by Mr Patten.

Such is the *Panglossian* tone of the White Paper that it ignores the clear danger of an educational underclass now emerging: of disappointed parents, rejected children and blighted schools. The White Paper appears to believe that a 'high quality common grounding' through the national curriculum is enough to ensure institutional equality. That fallacy was exposed in the 1950s. There is no parity between success and failure at eleven, only the hope that sensitive local planning can keep poorer schools up to the mark, postpone irrevocable decisions and guide parents and children through the maze. All this is now to pass to Whitehall.

There is a powerful case for further educational reform, not least in local school planning. But it cannot be right to go back to 1944, least of all on the basis of doubletalk about the contradictory concepts of parental choice and aptitude selection. British schools need time to recover from the inanities of the 1970s, not another blow of change – and certainly not a blow from the discredited sledgehammer of nationalisation.

Appendix 2
PATTEN'S DAD'S ARMY CAN'T SAVE OUR SCHOOLS

BARRY HUGILL

Barry Hugill, education correspondent of the Observer, *argues that the proposals in the Government's White Paper would 'nationalise' education and reduce the choice of parents (from the* Observer, *2 August 1992).*

'Parents know best the needs of their children,' declared last week's White Paper on education. 'Better than educational theorists or administrators, better even than our mostly excellent teachers,' it went on. But not, apparently, better than Mr John Patten.

The Secretary of State for Education has taken it upon himself to institute the most far-reaching blueprint for schools since R.A. Butler's famous Act of 1944. It took 'Rab' the best part of four years to prepare his legislation; Mr Patten has managed it in three months. The Butler Act served for nearly half a century; the Patten version will be lucky to survive five years.

The main reason why a new Education Act is needed is that parents, in their hundreds of thousands, have refused to do what Mr Kenneth Baker, the last but one pretender to Butler's crown, decreed they should do in his 1988 Education Act – an Act described at the time, incidentally, as the most far-reaching blueprint for schools since R.A. Butler's 1944 Act.

Mr Baker was confident that the majority of parents would insist on the schools their children attended opting out. He was wrong. So far, fewer than 300 state schools, out of over 24,000, have become grant maintained. So, to encourage the others, a new Act is required to change the rules to make it easier for them to opt out.

Both Mr Patten and Mr Baker pay lip-service to parental choice, yet between them they have instituted one of the most centralised, undemocratic and bureaucratic education systems in the Western world. So confident are they that parents really do know best that they have laid down by statute what every child, except those in the fee-paying sector, should learn, and at what age. Baker began, and Patten has completed, the nationalisation of our schools.

The architect of this new system, under which all schools will be controlled by Whitehall civil servants, their curricula decreed by a new quango staffed by men and women hand-picked by the Secretary of State on the basis of ideological correctness, and monitored by inspectors who put in the cheapest tenders, was not Mr Baker, but Mr Neil Kinnock.

In the early 1980s, when he was Shadow Education Secretary, Kinnock was shocked at the low standards he saw in some schools and decided that education was too important to be left to local councils. He toyed with the idea of stripping power away from those councils which failed to meet certain standards.

Rather as Mr Patten envisages retired headteachers forming 'hit squads' to take over failing schools, Mr Kinnock saw panels of experts charged with the task. His idea was short-lived because the powerful Labour local government lobby tore it to ribbons. The Shadow Education Secretary jokingly called it 'the Romanian model'. The joke was not lost on those around Kinnock, who rightly pointed out what fun the press would have with the plan were it ever to see the light of day.

Yet now, twelve years on, we have a Conservative Government planning to replace elected local education authorities with unaccountable education quangos. In future, the Minister will have the power to remove governors of schools that run into difficulties; to demand the closure of schools with falling rolls or to insist that others increase their numbers; to decide whether or not a school can bring back the Eleven-Plus. He will have powers never before held by an Education Secretary – and all in the name of extending parental choice and reducing local council bureaucracy.

Perhaps the most significant section of the White Paper, and the one least commented upon, is that dealing with surplus places. The Treasury is insisting firm action be taken to reduce the 1.5 million surplus school places and is angry that local councils have dragged their feet. A major reason for this is that schools faced with closure usually apply to opt out. Now the Minister will have unprecedented power to close schools, in defiance of governors and parents if he feels so inclined.

Closure of schools can mean but one thing – a reduction of parental choice. As competition for places becomes more acute, as it must, heads and governors will be in a powerful position to decide who gets a place. This is how selection will be reintroduced.

Some schools will opt for the old Eleven-Plus, but others will use more sophisticated techniques. Primary school reports will be assiduously studied; parents, and children, will be interviewed to judge 'aptitude'. However it is done, it will be the schools, not the parents, who do the choosing.

It would be unfair to blame Mr Patten for creating the conditions that give rise to sink schools. It is perfectly fair, however, to observe that his proposals are likely to make the situation worse, not better. The plan to send in 'hit squads', to be called educational associations, made up of 'retired teachers and people good at running things', is simply comical.

The key to a good school is a strong head, motivated teachers, adequate funding and involved parents. A Dads' Army of retired heads and former managers from industry with time on their hands is not going to perform miracles. Failing schools need experienced inspectors and advisers to point out the mistakes and draw up strategies. The Government, however, is keen to curtail the inspectorate and place monitoring in the hands of privatised inspection teams which will have to tender for work. The best that can be said for the Dads' Armies is they'll come cheap.

Over thirteen years of Conservative government by far the best Secretary of State was the much-missed John MacGregor, who won the respect of teachers, heads and administrators by not tinkering with the system. He didn't produce a White Paper or an Education Act, but set about trying to make Kenneth Baker's 'reforms' work. Mrs Thatcher considered he had gone soft and removed him.

For years our Education Ministers, MacGregor excluded, have searched for people to blame for low standards. Teachers, unions, local councils, professors, teacher trainers, sociologists, 'real book' enthusiasts, vice-chancellors, school inspectors, have had the finger pointed at them. Our schools were not good enough, and everyone was to blame except the Government. The current joke in education circles goes as follows: Question – What do you get when you read DFE (Department for Education) in the politically correct, i.e., phonetic, way? Answer – Deaf Ear.

The most urgent task for the next few years is to devise a sixteen to nineteen system to compare with those of our major economic competitors. Now that Mr Patten has nationalised schools, he can hardly blame other people if we fail to provide the skills training that is taken for granted in mainland Europe. Perhaps he will stop tinkering and start listening. If ever there was a need for consensus, it is now.

Appendix 3

THE ROLE OF GOVERNMENT IN EDUCATION

SIR MALCOLM THORNTON

Chairman of the House of Commons Select Committee on Education, Science and the Arts, Sir Malcolm Thornton is Conservative MP for Crosby, Liverpool. He was earlier a member of the Education Committee of the Association of Metropolitan Authorities and Chairman in 1978-79. He was also Chairman of the Council of Local Education Authorities in 1978.

We reproduce here the striking address Sir Malcolm gave on 3 December 1992 to a meeting of headteachers and academics at De Montfort University at Leicester, in which he claimed that ministers would have done better to have called a halt to further reforms after the 1988 Education Act. But, as the Times Educational Supplement *put it, he*

> *reserved his most trenchant criticism for the way in which ministers had allowed themselves to be unduly influenced by right-wing pressure groups which he defines as 'lords of misrule' and purveyors of 'insidious propaganda' (TES, 4 December 1992).*

We are grateful to Sir Malcolm, and to the De Montfort University, Leicester, for permission to reproduce this address at short notice.

I first stood for Parliament in the 1979 General Election. The greatest applause I received at any of my campaign meetings was in answer to a question from the floor. 'What new laws would you like to make?' I replied, 'None! Let's unmake a few first!'. I subscribe very firmly to the view that the best Government is that which governs least.

It is with some trepidation, therefore, that I address my remarks tonight to the role of the Government in Education. I do not think that there has been any time since the passing of the 1870 Elementary Education Act when the debate has raged so fiercely about the Government's role nor a time when so many fundamental questions are being asked about some of the underlying assumptions and assertions which are shaping current education policy.

For 27 years, first as a councillor and now, since 1979, as a Member of Parliament, I have been actively involved in the education system. For the past 18 years, I have been Chairman of Governors of Liscard Primary School in Wallasey – one of the largest primary schools in the country with over seven hundred pupils. From 1974 until I entered Parliament, I was a member of the A.M.A. Education Committee, becoming Chairman in 1978, a member of CLEA during much of the same period, becoming Chairman in 1978 – the AMA's 'turn' – and, for my sins, a member of the management panel of Burnham. How well I remember those dashes from Church House to Elizabeth House to try to extract an extra ½ per cent from Shirley Williams whilst Fred Jarvis and Terry Casey carried on their own private battles in the corridor!

I mention this – not to be immodest – but to illustrate the point that I entered the House with considerable experience of the education system at both local and national level – an experience which I naively thought might have been of use to someone, somewhere. After all, in the six months preceding the General Election, Mark Carlisle – then Opposition spokesman – seldom made any speech without first seeking my input.

I was in for a rude awakening. After the May election victory, the phone stopped ringing! New advice from new advisers was the order of the day. Although the voice of the LEAs – then solidly Conservative – was still listened to, it marked, in my view, the start of a process of disengagement which gathered pace slowly in the early 1980s and progressively increased to where we are today as we contemplate the effects of the present Bill.

Until recently, the progress of legislation since the Forster Act has emphasised and reinforced the position of the education service as 'a national service, locally administered'. Indeed, the 1888 Local Government Act – which created county councils and county borough councils – set the framework for LEAs which were established by the Balfour Act of 1902.

This Act marked the start of National Government's acceptance of the need not just for LEA *management* of the system but also for LEA *input*. The new LEAs took over the responsibility to provide adequate facilities for elementary education and, additionally, were authorised to provide 'education other than elementary', either by setting up new secondary schools or by aiding existing ones in their area. They were allowed – within set limits – to raise and spend rates to fulfil these responsibilities. Not surprisingly, there was great disparity of provision!

Between 1902 and 1918, a judicious mix of enabling and prescriptive legislation – there were only three Acts of any significance – moved further down the road of LEA involvement. The Fisher Act of 1918, with its requirement that LEAs should submit schemes of development, set out to ensure that a fully national system of public education was being set up. It also further extended the powers of LEAs by allowing them to set up nursery schools or classes. Once again, unsurprisingly, disparity of provision resulted.

The Butler Act of 1944 laid the foundations for the modern education system. It replaced nearly all earlier education legislation and was, I believe, the fruits of balanced judgement of the developments and thinking which had been taking place over the years – particularly since the 1918 Act. Significantly, it gave the Minister of Education a creative rather than just a controlling function – charging him or her with promoting education.

To pretend that all this was achieved by universal agreement would be foolish. Of course there were criticisms. Of course, standards of attainment were questioned. Of course, more expansion of services meant more money and of course, that money was not always provided by either national or local government. But I do believe that it *was* achieved by a remarkable consensus – where the role of the Government in setting the framework and its interface with LEAs and those working in the system was readily understood and accepted. However – as I shall be referring later to others whose attitudes to education seem to be based on the notion of a long-past, greatly lamented 'golden age' – I do not want to stand accused of the same charge where political attitudes are concerned.

If the Butler Act changed the face of Education, then so, too, was the political face of this country changed in the aftermath of War. Slowly but surely over the following twenty years or so, party political influences were seeping into educational thinking at every level. Instead of evolution, which produced the Butler Act, revolution seemed to be the order of the day. The sound of political axes being sharpened could be heard throughout the land. Other axes, too, were being similarly honed. As the political profile of education was being raised, Chief Education Officers, teachers and all who are lumped into that awful phrase 'the education establishment' – to which I shall return later – saw their chance to capitalise on this changing scene.

Therein lay the seeds of much of today's polarisation and prejudice. To be for or against a piece of legislation or a circular which owed its origins more to party political dogma than to sound educational thinking was to declare one's allegiance to that Party's policies. A week may well be a long time in politics, but old memories die hard and old scores remain to be settled. More of that, too, later!

Without any doubt, the single issue which provoked the greatest degree of political and educational polarisation was the move towards comprehensive secondary education. The political parties nailed their colours to the mast and went for broke. Never mind the real debate which had been taking place – again, I am tempted to use the word 'evolution' – the great and the good on each side sailed into a battle which rages on to this day.

I have to confess that I have not stood totally on the outside of this argument. I, too, believed that the tri-partite system was all that was right and, conversely, that comprehensive schools would only serve to 'level down'. After all, wasn't I a product of the grammar school system? Didn't it give me the opportunity of a quality of education which my parents could not have afforded to buy for me? Indeed it did and I am grateful for it. A combination of reasonable ability in certain subjects, academic laziness and a passion for sport gave me five years of highly enjoyable secondary education. I did not see – at that age, why should I have been? – the problems in the 'C' forms as I moved up through the school.

It was only in later years that I began to ask some of the real questions about those days – questions not just about the under-achievers at the grammar schools but also questions about other schools in the system. It is ironic that many of those who shout the loudest about the ability of our education system to produce such a high proportion of under-achievers are at the same time the greatest advocates of a return to a system which – if it had been left unchanged – tended to institutionalise it. A large part of the debate revolves around this question of change. Clearly, a highly-selective school can benefit the best. But what about the rest? I do not believe that there is any one pure orthodoxy which can claim, conclusively, to have won the argument. Diversity – a word we have all come to recognise immediately – should be an essential agreement.

But to allow diversity is not to guarantee automatically the qualitative improvements which everyone seeks. A fundamental change in attitude has to be the first step. As long as 'parity of esteem' remains as merely words on paper and not part of the wider public consciousness, the problem will remain.

I shall illustrate this by what I call 'the grand piano syndrome'. The local secondary-modern had been asking for a replacement piano. The one they had had been tuned to extinction and only half the notes played anyway! After repeated requests, over several years, the local education committee, following great deliberation, allowed them the money for a quite-good, second-hand piano. But the grammar school got a new grand piano!

This sort of attitude is still widespread. Parents, pupils, teachers, employers – a significant proportion of all these groups – will never make the quantum leap forward as long as politicians – and those who advise them – perpetuate the myths of the past. To believe otherwise is definitely a triumph of hope over experience. The failure lies on both sides. If those who advocate a selective system at school level – as distinct from selection within a school – had addressed the problems and needs of those pupils who were deemed failures, then the pressures for compulsory change would most certainly have diminished. And if those who condemn selection as divisive and educationally unsound – a somewhat narrow view to which I do not subscribe – had not so readily espoused the the political dimension of the debate, then the sort of evolutionary moves which had already started would, I suggest, have continued and spread. In the event, common sense has been thrown overboard and the debate has foundered on the rocks of dogma and disenchantment.

Before I turn specifically to the legislation of the past decade, I cannot leave this rather depressing part of my remarks without addressing two further points. Firstly, the 'education establishment'. Each of us here will have a clear idea in our own minds of what *we* think it is. I suspect that most of us would, in fact, agree. For others, it is not a phrase to be used in polite company! Whilst in some quarters it may be fashionable to use it as a convenient 'catch-all' for all those groups or individuals who are perceived – sometimes, I am bound to say, quite justifiably – to have some responsibility for problems and deficiencies in the system, its very nature as a 'catch-all' is an insult to all those who devote their efforts to achieving improvements in education at every level. It serves only to widen the gulf and risks alienating – if it has not already done so – those who want to work with the grain of reform in an essential partnership between the policy-makers and those who have to implement it.

My second point concerns those who view the past as some sort of golden age. For every field of human activity, there is always some element of nostalgia, some talk of the 'good old days'. Apart from the fact that such judgements are always highly subjective, they almost always ignore the inescapable fact that we do not live in some sort of time warp. Society has changed. Attitudes to authority, expectations, morality – all have changed. We may wish that some had not – but to pretend that the changes can be reversed is to ignore reality and the lessons which history teaches us.

The education system does not exist in a vacuum. It, too, reflects the changes which have taken place in society and has had to respond to the pressures of those changes. But alongside this has gone innovation and development from within education itself. Exciting concepts for learn-ing and a greater degree of pupil participation in the process of learning have been a feature in many primary schools. LEAs, using their enabling powers, have been at the forefront in developing programmes of training and development for teachers – expanding their horizons beyond the confines of their own individual classrooms and schools.

There is, of course, so much more that I could say. To be proud of these achievements and to acknowledge the undoubted benefits derived from them by children should not, however, disguise the fact that the balance between rigour and the wider aspects of learning has been allowed to slip in certain schools. In too many cases the disparity in provision – in every sense of the word – had become indefensible. Left to themselves, schools and colleges are not always the best judges of their own performance. I see nothing wrong, therefore, in using national standards for making these assessments – always providing that such benchmarks are set *after* proper consideration and the widest consul-tation. There is, of course, one further criterion which must be met. They must actually work! To this end, it does seem sensible to take note of the comments of those who have to administer whatever form of testing or assessment is deemed necessary. Perhaps this is a classic example of where it is the proper role of Government to fix the principle – and then leave the implementation to the professionals in the field.

Throughout the 1980s, the Government's role in education has been far more prescriptive than enabling. I believe, in many cases, this to have been right. From the 1980 Act onwards, choice, parental involvement and diversity have figured prominently both in the legislation itself as well as in the rhetoric surrounding it. In this Act, certain rights were given to parents – a right to choose the school they wanted their child to go to – a right to be represented on school governing bodies – a right to receive information from LEAs and school governors on admission policies, exam results, curriculum, discipline and organisation.

This was welcome indeed. It gave legislative force to the need for partnership between home and school and opened up doors which for too long had been either locked against parents or, at best, grudgingly opened for their inspection. It also raised parental expectations – expectations which were not always realised, particularly where choice of schools was concerned.

The 1980 Act also set up the Assisted Places Scheme as a replacement for the Direct Grant system which had been scrapped by the Labour government. Whatever criticisms may be levelled at this scheme, it was always more than just a lifeline thrown to independent schools. It offered opportunities to many children to benefit from a type of education which was not universally available within the state sector. It did, indeed, give some diversity in the system.

Before moving on to the 1986 and 1988 Acts, I should like to use the 1981 Act – widely known as the Warnock Act – as an example of both Government sucess and Government failure. By responding to a debate which had been going on for some considerable time, Government succeeded, by willing the ends – i.e. a legislative framework. By not recognising the financial implications of the legislation, Government failed, by not willing the means – i.e. the extra resources which were always implicit therein.

I sat on the Committee stage. It was set up as a Special Committee, in that the first three sessions were conducted under Select Committee procedures. Chaired by the then Select Committee Chairman, the Committee took evidence before the usual consideration of the Bill. (I am bound to say, I should like to see this happen again!). There was almost total unanimity at every stage. I can well remember the positive feelings I had at the time. All of us felt that we had contributed to a piece of legislation which would have significant beneficial effects on those children whose needs were so specific.

The 1981 Act gave an impetus to the move to integrate children with special needs into mainstream schools. The success story of the past decade has been the integration of children with physical and sensory handicaps into mainstream schools: adaptations, both to buildings and the curriculum; more support by welfare helpers and nursery nurses for individual children; more children with visual and hearing impairments being supported in mainstream classes and fewer in segregated units and schools; all these – and more – have been achieved without any direction or special funding from the DFE. There have been no special grants for adaptations to schools, no recognition that it is more expensive to support such children in mainstream schools; no government studies of the success, or otherwise, of the move towards integration or its pace.

Central government has a number of mechanisms which it can use to stimulate change in education, ranging from advice on good practice and guidance to regulation and direction. The Department has used education support grants to support specific projects with tightly defined criteria. But there has been no lead on the most important issues in special education since the passage of the 1981 Act; no lead on the definition of special educational needs – this was noted in the Audit Commission/HMI Report – and no lead on strategies for integration. My Select Committee has just started an inquiry into the way in which 'statementing' – as defined by the 1981 Act – is working. We have already taken evidence from Baroness Warnock. Admittedly using the advantages of hindsight, she has concluded that perhaps we were all a little naive to have been so optimistic.

A further move towards increasing the role of Government in the detail of education was made in the 1984 Education (Grants & Awards) Act. This allowed the Government to allocate sums of money to LEAs for particular educational purposes. This reserved money was offered in the form of education support grants of up to 75 per cent of the cost of each project, in areas which the Secretary of State deemed to be important. This did, of course, reduce local authorities' control over how the block grant is spent. I have no quarrel with this. It seems to me to be absolutely justified for any Secretary of State to insist that certain monies – which he will have had to wring out of the Treasury – are actually spent on those priorities which he considers appropriate. If only we could have won this argument at the time of the Warnock Bill!

The second of the two Education Acts of 1986 further entrenched the role of governors vis-a-vis LEAs and gave significant new powers for parents. The formula which was set for representation on each governing body increased parental influence, weakened that of LEAs and widened the use of co-opted members. The Act required the governors to present an annual report to parents and to arrange a meeting to discuss it. In short, it was giving schools and their governing bodies more responsibilities as well as more autonomy.

I believe the *educational* case for this was sound. It gave a healthy balance between the powers of the LEA and the ability of a school to have a greater say over its own affairs. It made governors take their responsibilities more seriously and it made parents much more aware of their role in the partnership between school and home. It forced LEAs to be much more forthcoming over matters such as admission policies, repairs and maintenance as well as politically sensitive matters such as sex education policy.

However, the *political* case which was being made in certain quarters was a matter of concern. Siren voices – then still muted, but gathering strength – advocated going very much further – breaking for ever the power and influence of LEAs and the education establishment – those words again! – which they saw as the main, if not the sole, culprits in the perceived failure in our schools. I have to confess that, although I heard these voices, I felt sure that common sense would prevail and that it would be alright in the end. *Mea culpa!*

At this point, it is worth reflecting on exactly how these new powers affected the attitudes as well as the role of parents. As a chairman of governors, I was immediately delighted with the interest shown and the input made by the parent-governors. They added a significant extra dimension to our discussions and the improved knowledge of parental hopes and fears by the staff was a genuine bonus. The annual meeting was quite a different matter. Talking to colleagues, I discover that my experience was by no means unique. Only a handful of parents bothered to turn up. On 90 per cent of occasions, governors and staff constituted 90 per cent of the audience. The other occasions when a larger number attended were always when there was a matter of particular controversy or concern. Again, this reflected experience elsewhere and, sadly, is still the case.

I mention this to illustrate the reasons why I, personally, am a little sceptical of the belief that 'parental power' is the sole key to significant progress in the improvement of education. This, I readily accept, is not only an unfashionable view in political circles – on both sides, I must add! – but will be considered by some as heresy. I make no apologies. Parents *have* a vital role to play. They are the first educators of their children. They have an absolute right to know what is going to happen to those children when they go to school. Without a genuine 'home/school' partnership, achievement will be measurably reduced. They have a right to expect schools and teachers to meet their reasonable expectations. They should be given as much choice as possible. They should have a say in the running of their children's schools.

But just as choice is most definitely limited, so the increased rights of parents have to be set firmly alongside parental responsibilities. Again, the key word is partnership – a mutual recognition by parents and teachers of the part each group has to play in the way in which children progress – or not – through their schooldays. Neither parent nor teacher 'always knows best'. With their unique knowledge of their children, parents will always have something quite special to contribute. As trained professionals, committed and experienced as most are, so, too, do teachers.

The role of government in all this is critical. The expectations raised by the Parents Charter need to be matched by much greater emphasis and explanation by Ministers of where responsibilities *ultimately* rest and of the crucial importance of parents and professionals working together.

Almost as an aside, I should just like to say how delighted I was when, in 1987, the Teachers' Pay and Conditions Act swept into history the unloved Burnham machinery. Although it took another four years before the 1991 Act set up the Review Body for which I and many others had been asking for many years, I believe these two pieces of legislation marked a significant step forward in the way Government viewed the teaching profession. I hope you will forgive if I do not go down the rather rougher road of a pay review body of a different kind!

In a speech in, I believe, Birmingham in 1986, Eric Bolton said that the establishment of a National Curriculum was the most significant step forward in education since the 1870 Elementary Education Act. Few would disagree, I venture to suggest. The 1988 Education Reform Act empowered the Secretary of State to prescribe a common curriculum for pupils of compulsory school age in maintained schools, to set attainment targets for each of its constituent subjects at the ages of 7, 11, 14 and 16 and to make arrangements for assessing how well these are met. The Act established a National Curriculum Council and required LEAs, school governors and headteachers to ensure that the national curriculum is taught in all maintained schools. It is this part of the Act that I shall address first.

A broad consensus lay behind the establishment of the National Curriculum. Although there was always a lack of total unanimity concerning both the precise content and the weighting given to individual subjects, it was seen as a genuine tool for improving overall standards of attainment and of putting an end to what many saw as the unco-ordinated, unstructured and, occasionally, incoherent way in which schools had developed. My own favourite expression is educational drift!

Inevitably, this meant a massive upheaval in schools. Equally inevitably, there were some from within education who resented the imposition but I firmly believe that they were in a minority. Married as I am to a primary school headteacher and wearing my hat as Chairman of Governors, I know how enthusiastic most teachers were at the time – seeing an opportunity which challenged them professionally and promised so much good for the children in their care. There were, of course, many more reservations expressed about testing – the SATs. Many teachers felt that the tests would tell them little they did not already know. However, I was persuaded – and still am – that some form of measurement, decided nationally, is an essential part of the rigour needed in a modern education system. I am less happy about the use of which the results of those tests are put.

Another major requirement of the Act was the delegation by LEAs of certain responsibilities for financial and staff matters to governing bodies. It also permitted the governing body to delegate many of these responsibilities to the headteacher. The underlying principle was that such delegation would give schools greater *freedom* over the use of their resources and increase the *overall* amount of those resources by reducing centralised bureaucracy. It would allow LEAs to concentrate more of their efforts on major policy issues. It would also ensure that certain monies were retained at the centre for the provision of services which, by any definition, could best be provided by the LEA on behalf of all schools.

Liscard Primary School was a 'pilot' for the scheme of delegation Overall, we found far more advantages than disadvantages although the learning curve was steep indeed. Perhaps most significantly, we were able to use a substantial amount of senior staff time, a luxury that subsequently could not be afforded, as budgets have been squeezed. The reality is that the administrative load, as far as day to day matters are concerned, falls increasingly on the headteacher.

The Coopers and Lybrand Report to the DFE on Local Management of Schools set out very fully the advantages as well as areas of potential difficulty. In the Report's summary, two comments are worthy of note: 'To implement LMS across the country will not be cheap. It will require both staff time and cash.' Further on it states, 'Nor do we think that the implementation of LMS can be rushed: attitudes take time to change.'

I have no doubt that the basic principle of delegation is right. I am equally sure that the comments from the Report which I have just quoted are right. So what has gone wrong? Quite simply, the *effects* of delegation on individual schools' budgets combined with all other financial pressures on both local authorities and schools were not thought through. Undoubtedly, many schools are finding that, through no fault of their own, their budgets have been reduced and the quality of the education which they are able to deliver is suffering. To be told that you have the freedom to choose is a sick joke when the only choice is between losing a teacher or slashing an already reduced sum for capitation. Too many headteachers are spending far too much of their time wrestling with their budgets and far too little on developing the educational ethos of their schools. A recent newspaper survey demonstrated just how pervasive this has become. I cannot believe that this was the intention of the legislation.

Although the 1988 Act contained highly significant matters affecting Higher and Further Education – matters of considerable importance to many here this evening – I have quite deliberately confined my remarks to schools.

It is in our schools that the process of formalised learning starts. It is at schools that the bulk of legislation has been directed. It is schools that are under attack for the perceived fall in standards. It is from schools that colleges and universities get their students. It is to schools that parents and employers look for young people with the basic skills and learning to carry them through life and into work.

Many of you will have noticed that I have not yet mentioned that part of the 1988 Act which allowed schools to become grant-maintained. In my remarks thus far, I have tried to deal with the role of the Government against the background of legislation of which the *principles* were sound but where, in certain cases, neither had the consequences been fully considered nor the necessary resources provided.

The concept of grant-maintained schools owes more, in my view, to the antipathy of national government to local authorities than to finding the best way to improve education in this country. As one who has long advocated either the total ring-fencing of the schools' budget or central funding for all schools, I certainly do not believe that the old order should go on unchanged. The reservations which I expressed at the time – reservations concerning the compatibility of the then Reform Bill with other legislation and the disproportionate effect which schools' 'opting out' would have on the LEAs' plans – have now been magnified.

I suspect that many people were surprised – I know I was – when the White Paper, 'Choice and Diversity' fell short of the widely-expected recommendation that LEAs were to be dispensed with – certainly as a channel for the funding of schools. Given the Government's stated objective of encouraging more and more schools to seek grant maintained status, surely the logic of their position points firmly in that direction. Instead we have, I believe, a recipe for, at best, confusion and at worst, chaos. If the LEAs are all so bad – and they're not! – then scrap them. Replace them with an area funding agency and make the transition as quick and clean as possible. If LEAs are to be retained, but in a different role, then define that role and spell out the alternative arrangements for funding. Simply to allow a sort of 'withering on the vine' is the worst of all worlds.

In his speech to the 1992 Conference of the Council for Local Education Authorities, Eric Bolton, formerly her Majesty's Chief Inspector of Schools, spoke of the need for a coherent vision and 'an underpinning theory, allied to a shared and generally accepted vision and philosophy'. In this area of such fundamental change to the organisation of our schools, I confess that I can see neither coherence nor vision. Very reluctantly, I have come to the conclusion that the anti-LA/LEA lobby have succeeded in persuading too many of my colleagues to believe that such authorities are the main obstacles in the way of progress towards an ideal with which no-one, surely, would disagree – namely, in the Prime Minister's own words – 'to secure what I believe to be essential – to ask the best *for* every child; to ask the best *from* very child. Excellence must be the key word in all our schools: that is what our children deserve.'

If only we could have drawn breath after the passing of the 1988 Act. There was a brief moment – under the charge of John MacGregor – when it looked as though that might happen. But that glimmer of light was snuffed out before most people realised it was there! From that point on, I believe that both the wider debate and the ears of Ministers have been disproportionately influenced by extremists – extremists whose pronouncements become ever wilder and further from the reality of the world of education which I recognize, in which I work and for which I care deeply.

And who are they to foist upon the children of this country ideas which will only serve to take them backwards? What hard evidence do they have to support their assertions? How often do they actually go into schools and see for themselves what is really happening? What possible authority can they claim for representing the views of 'the overwhelming majority of parents'? I believe that in all their answers to these – and many more – questions, they are found wanting.

Their insidious propaganda must be challenged. They seek to return to a world which, if it ever existed, cannot be recreated today. To do so would mean disinventing television and information technology; disregarding the massive social changes which have taken place, and so many other things which have not just changed society at large but also have had an enormous impact on our education system. What may have been possible 30 or 40 years ago is no longer – in large measure – a practical reality for today. You would not, I know, wish me to use hackneyed phrases or trite words such as 'rose-tinted spectacles' or 'backwoodsmen' to describe these lords of misrule. I will try to do better. The extreme right-wing think tanks – representing, I believe, the remnants of a group of people who, quite rightly, challenged many of the assumptions which had become entrenched in our education system, are the spindle and loom of chaos; the offspring of bigoted minds and muddy understandings. Sadly, whole sections of our nation, once respected for common sense, have been brainwashed into an acceptance of their dogma. Scarcely a day goes by without yet another newspaper article giving them credibility. Broad brushstrokes and sweeping statements and the use of extreme, individual examples where things have gone badly wrong are all they use to justify their dangerous creed. I am not an immoderate man. I am frequently astonished by my moderation! I could not, however, let this occasion pass without standing up for the voices of sanity and experience in education and by speaking out against those whose plans, if left unchecked, will, I believe, ensure that the Government's own stated objectives for the qualitative improvement of education in this country will remain further off than ever.

So what should be the role of the Government in our education system? Clearly, it has a legislative function – to set the framework. In this, Government has the enormous responsibility of getting it right! This may be to state the obvious but, given the length of time it takes for change to work through the system, ill-considered legislation is like a time-bomb – ticking away and set to explode, perhaps many years later. Others then will have to pick up the pieces but, in the meantime, a generation of children will have been affected.

It is, therefore, of critical importance that, before legislation is even contemplated, Government decides *where* it wants to get to and *how* it can best get there. It must balance legitimate political objectives with the views of those in the field. It must accept the resource implications of proposed changes. Quality does not come either cheaply or automatically. It must recognise those areas – such as teacher-training – where significant steps can be taken. It must recognise, too, that the pace of change needs carefully controlling. The school day and timetable is not made of elastic. The administrative overload in many schools today is threatening to engulf them.

At the heart of my job as Chairman of an All-Party Select Committee, is the absolute imperative of trying to find a balance between differing views – views often deeply entrenched. Select Committees have to find a way forward based on a willingness to listen to others' opinions and 'give and take' is a prerequisite of a successful report. Consensus should not be seen as weakness but as a means of achieving progress. Surely, it is better to move forward together, by consent, than risk losing everything by polarising the discussion throughout. In the field of education, a high level of consent is vital. Without it, all the legislation in the world will not bring about the significant improvements desired by everyone.

All concerned in education could do worse than to reflect upon Francis Parkman's words in 'The Tale of the Ripe Scholar': 'To direct popular education, not to stuffing the mind with crude aggregations of imperfect knowledge, but rather to the development of its powers of observation, comparison, analysis and reasoning; to strengthening and instructing its moral sense and leading it to self-knowledge and consequent modesty'.

For many years, schools the length and breadth of the land have been responding to the challenge of those words – moving along an evolutionary path that builds on the best practice, seeks to eliminate weaknesses and recognizes – perhaps above all else – that our education system must adapt and change in order to reflect and meet the changes all around us.

Government must respond, too. Goethe's assertion, 'Divide and rule, a good motto. Unite and lead, a better one!' seems particularly appropriate. Where legislation has worked best, it has worked because of a widely-held belief that *all* views had been considered beforehand – surely the essence of a partnership without which the aims of Government will simply not be realised. It is not Ministers who deliver the improvements in standards. In the final analysis, it is the teachers in our schools who will bring this about. The re-establishment of this partnership is critical. The gulf which has opened up between the professionals and many politicans threatens so much of what *can* be achieved – of what *must* be achieved.

We pride ourselves on being an enlightened country. Why is it, in a land so full of enlightenment, there are so many who cannot see?

SUBJECT INDEX

Name Index